AT THE Mercy
OF THE Sea

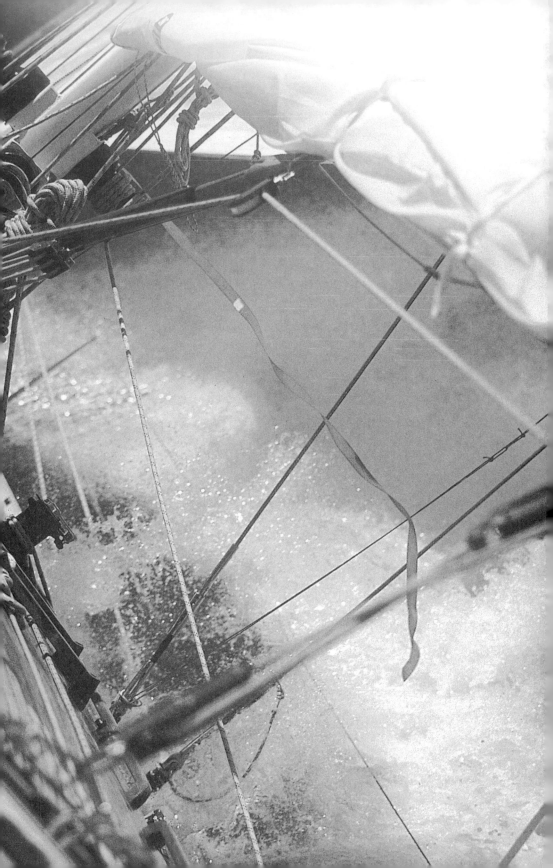

JOHN KRETSCHMER

AT THE Mercy OF THE Sea

THE TRUE STORY
OF THREE SAILORS
IN A CARIBBEAN
HURRICANE

International Marine / McGraw-Hill
Camden, Maine • New York • Chicago • San Francisco • Lisbon
London • Madrid • Mexico City • Milan • New Delhi • San Juan
Seoul • Singapore • Sydney • Toronto

The **McGraw·Hill** Companies

1 2 3 4 5 6 7 8 9 DOC DOC 9 8 7 6

Library of Congress Cataloging-in-Publication Data

Kretschmer, John.
  At the mercy of the sea : the true story of three sailors in a caribbean hurricane / John Kretschmer.
     p. cm.
  ISBN 0-07-147507-9 (hardcover : alk. paper)
  1. Sailing—Caribbean Area—Anecdotes. 2. Heavy weather seamanship.
  3. Boating accidents—Caribbean Area. 4. Kretschmer, John,—Travel—Caribbean Area. I. Title.
  GV817.C37K74 2007
  797.12409729—dc22   2006017415

ISBN-13: 978-0-07-147507-5
ISBN-10: 0-07-147507-9

Maps by International Mapping.
Photo pages ii–iii by Imagestock.

To my mother, Jeanne Kretschmer

CONTENTS

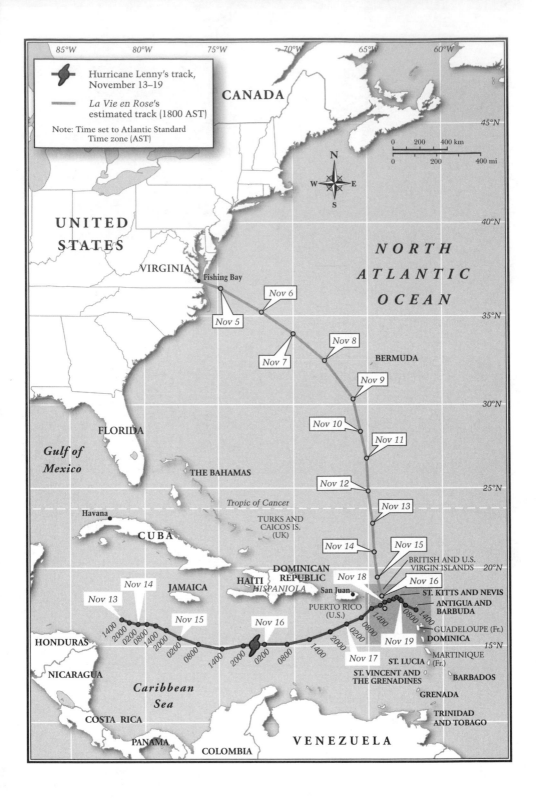

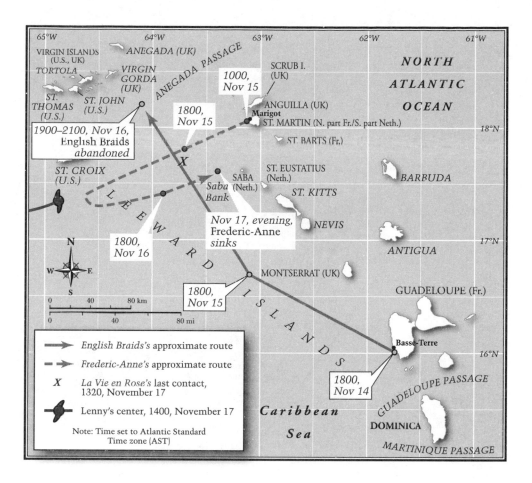

AT THE Mercy
OF THE Sea

PROLOGUE: ABBEVILLE

"But it was another thought that visited Brother Juniper: 'Why did this happen to those five?' If there were any plan in the universe at all, if there were any pattern in a human life, surely it could be discovered mysteriously latent in those lives so suddenly cut off. Either we live by accident and die by accident, or we live by plan and die by plan. And on that instant Brother Juniper made the resolve to inquire into the secret lives of those five persons."

Thornton Wilder, *The Bridge of San Luis Rey*

I WAS unusually nervous as I stood to speak. The funeral home chapel was simple, well lit, and generically ornamented to offend no Christian, even a lapsed one. It was almost cheery. But I was feeling unsettled on that drizzly November morning in the South Carolina hill country. Shifting my feet and trying not to stare at the flag-draped casket, even then, just days after my friend Carl Wake had been fished out of the faraway Caribbean, I sensed a deeper tragedy beyond the immediate sadness.

Carl's people were hoping that I might offer some insight into what had happened, how his grand plan to sail the oceans of the world had been prematurely snuffed out by a wrong-way hurricane. Perhaps they hoped I could make some sense of his death and explain why it hadn't been for nothing. My voice was shaky as I told the small gathering that I had known Carl only three years. I said that I knew him as a friend, as a dreamer, and as a sailor, which I believed

I

was about the best way to know anybody. I said that I understood the spirit of his quest as well as I understood anything in life.

I tried to continue, but no recognizable words left my mouth, which was probably a good thing. I knew—and I'm sure many of them did too—that the motivations for his voyage were tangled. They ranged from the familiar desire to escape society's shackles, to a lurking resentment about the life cards he'd been dealt, to cautious hopes for happier days beyond the horizon. At age 53 he had stood alone with his fragile dreams.

The dreams of the young are white-hot. Given the slightest encouragement, they burn like wildfire. The young are stopped by lack of means, rarely by lack of dreams. But Carl was not a brash young man with reckless visions. He had been dreaming his last dream, not his first, and it takes an effort of will to summon one last dream when so many have turned sour. Carl had means but no illusions; he was old enough to have learned, in the poet Donald Justice's words, to close softly the doors to rooms he would not be coming back to. His greatest advantage was his acute awareness that he had no time left for procrastination.

I chose not to explain to Carl's family and friends that his death was haunting me. I had been one of Carl's sailing mentors, one of the so-called experts he relied on. I had helped him find his boat and talked him into buying it. I had given him a two-bit pep talk on the phone the day before he shoved off on his fateful singlehanded passage from the Chesapeake Bay to the Caribbean islands. I had been scheduled to sail to the islands a week later, and we had planned a rendezvous in St. Thomas. I didn't tell his teary-eyed nephew and silent niece how I had ignored the anxiety and weariness in his voice, or how he had lingered on the line. Pressed for time, I had assured him that everything would be fine.

"The forecast looks good," I had told him with thinly disguised impatience, "and the tropics are clear. You've got yourself a nice weather window." Then, in a big-brother tone the memory of which will always make me cringe, I reminded him that fatigue, not weather, was his chief concern. "It doesn't matter when you get to St. Thomas, just that you do get there. If you want a goal, make it before Thanksgiving so you can buy me dinner. Take it easy, Carl. Suck the marrow out of the experience. This is what you've been dreaming about. Don't forget to eat and sleep. Have a great passage. I'll see you in about three weeks, amigo."

When I did see him three weeks later, he was in a coffin, and I was angry, heartbroken, awash with guilt. It seemed profoundly unfair that Hurricane Lenny had picked a fight with Carl. Lenny was a bully of a tempest, Carl the new kid in school. Seeking partly to assuage my conscience and partly to understand how this calamity could have occurred, I resolved to find out all I could about the details of Carl's first and last blue-water passage. I became obsessed with the minutiae of how he must have spent his final hours afloat, battling conditions that were beyond surviving, conditions that would have mocked the stoutest sailor, the stoutest little boat, the stoutest dream. As I pieced together bits of information and reconstructed his passage, I began to see that you can sail away from your life ashore, but you can't sail away from yourself.

The spare outline of what had happened was haunting, but soon I learned that there was more to the story. I discovered that Carl had not been the only character in what turned out to be a three-act tragedy. Although he had set off on his fateful voyage single-handed, Carl wasn't alone when he died. Three men perished in the heart of the storm. The three had shared a bond of sailing, but in other ways they were as different from one another as men could be. They were from three countries, sailing three fundamentally different boats, heading in three different directions on the chart and in life. None had any idea of the others' existence until a hurricane tossed them together.

Each man thought he was doing the right thing, following his gut instincts, trying to skirt the swirling madness, fighting for his life. Drawn unwaveringly into the maelstrom like moths to a lamp, they converged in the lair of a Cyclops, a one-eyed monster named Lenny. And within the howling walls of that lethal vortex, Carl Wake found a last chance for redemption.

I didn't know any of this as I stood unsteadily next to my friend. I had only just returned from the waters that had claimed his life. The whims of a dictator had spared me my own encounter with Lenny. What I did know, and what I finally managed to mumble to his loved ones, was that my life was richer for having known Carl.

TRADE WINDS

"There is, one knows not what sweet mystery about this sea,
whose gently awful stirrings seem to speak of some hidden
soul beneath."

Herman Melville, Moby-Dick

NAUTICAL twilight, that sanguine half hour between
dark and light, when Venus lingers a couple of fists above the
horizon and the clouds foretell what the gods are conjuring, is
the best time of day for singlehanded sailors. The long night
vigil, the battle to keep your eyelids propped open, is over, at
least for a few hours. The terrors withdraw that lurked all night
beyond the tiny circle of your navigation lights—the derelict
shipping containers, the pale beasts swimming up from the
ocean depths, the memories and hallucinations swimming up
from your subconscious. A cup of coffee, a bowl of cereal, a
glance at the chart, a quick survey of the deck, and all is well in
your floating universe. Anxiety gives way to confidence.
Daylight after an all-night watch delivers a powerful dose of
energy. From the perspective of a small-boat cockpit, beyond
sight and scent of land, the life-sustaining powers of the rising
sun are palpable.

Sunday morning, November 14, 1999, treated the one-man
crew of the 42-foot sailboat *La Vie en Rose* to a reassuring sunrise. Not a trace of red tinged the sky. The trade winds were

fitful but had been filling in nicely during the past couple of days. Carl Wake, skipper, navigator, cook, and chief bottle washer of his floating domain and enterprise, could almost smell 20 knots of fresh breeze ahead. *La Vie en Rose*'s course lay southward. She'd battled east and then southeast, leaving the capricious zephyrs and annoying squalls of the horse latitudes behind. She'd crossed the all-important 65th meridian, dubbed I-65 by cruising sailors. Running from pole to pole, stretching through Nova Scotia and Tierra del Fuego, this imaginary line of longitude pierces two vital waypoints for North Atlantic sailors, Bermuda and the Virgin Islands.

Carl's web log entry records that *La Vie en Rose* was on a sweet reach, driven at nearly 6 knots over shimmering seas by the wind blowing over her port shoulder. Carl was content to let the autopilot handle the steering. He was just over 200 miles from his destination, St. Thomas, in the U.S. Virgin Islands. At her current pace *La Vie en Rose* was less than two days from landfall, her skipper less than two days from a full night's sleep.

Ever since putting his lumbering golden retriever ashore a few months earlier, Carl noted in his log with a touch of concern, he'd been talking to himself, to his boat, to the petrels, to Neptune, to anyone or anything that might listen. He needed to hear his voice, it seemed. "Good morning, Atlantic Ocean!" he bellowed, imitating Robin Williams's rant from the movie *Good Morning, Vietnam.* "And you too, *La Vie.*" Carl was nearly nine days outbound from the Chesapeake Bay. He had sailed toward Bermuda, flirting with a landfall there, but the weather forecast had been favorable, he was making decent progress, and he had finally found his rhythm. Suddenly a Bermuda landfall had seemed more hassle than haven. He had turned right and pressed on for the Caribbean islands, and now Bermuda was an afterthought, three hard sailing days astern.

Carl would have loved Bermuda. The postcard-perfect, easy-to-enter harbor fronting St. George was framed by bougainvillea and crowded with cruising boats of every description. The "Dark and Stormies" and the sea stories flowed late into the night at the taverns along Somers Wharf. But Carl had never been to Bermuda. He carried clear and cherished pictures of the Virgin Islands on his cortex from having sailed there years before, but Bermuda was no more real or reassuring to him than words in a pilot guide. Had it been otherwise, all would have been different.

He was bone weary but still outwardly cheery. That was Carl's persona, his MO, one he sustained even when there was no one else around to fool. The thoughts percolating below the exterior charm were harder to pin down. He was a master of deception, even to himself. His decision to skip Bermuda now seemed validated, but the sea is not a place where boasting ever feels right, especially when a traveler is alone. A solo sailor is too vulnerable, and besides, few human endeavors are as exhausting as singlehanded sailing. Even an experienced single-hander can feel his strength ebbing through his pores with his sweat. It hurts to think. The wheels in his brain seem to bind up as if out of round, and he feels incredibly dim-witted. Day after day of 20-minute catnaps rocks a body's natural rhythms. And this was Carl's first genuine blue-water passage. But at least he was almost there. He'd sleep for a week once he arrived, and then, when he awoke, maybe he'd quietly congratulate himself.

Making a crude breakfast, Carl once again regretted not taking on fresh produce before leaving the marina in Fishing Bay, near the bottom of the Chesapeake Bay. He wrote in his log that he had enough canned food to feed a battalion, but nothing gets older than canned food day after day. When the press greeted famed solo sailor Robin Knox-Johnston on the dock in Plymouth, England, more than thirty years ago, the first man to sail nonstop around the world was asked what he would do differently if he were to do it again. "Bring something to eat other than 300 tins of corned beef," he replied. New sailors often underestimate the value, both to body and to soul, of good food at sea. Carl had lived aboard for a year and a half and messed about in boats since he was a kid, but by the uncompromising standards of the sea he was still a new sailor. He poured himself another bowl of cereal, splashed it with powdered milk, and longed for a piece of fruit.

Carl ate standing up, bracing himself in the small galley, swaying naturally to the rhythm of the boat. *La Vie en Rose* had a soft motion in a seaway. She didn't pound into waves; she sliced through them without confrontation, the mark of a good sea boat. She rolled a bit from side to side when running before a following sea, the result of her relatively narrow beam, slack bilges, deep keel, and heavy lead ballast, but those same features made her seaworthy when the ocean turned unruly. Carl tossed his bowl into the sink and poked his head out the companionway. Carl and I had talked often about how to maintain a safe watch as a singlehander, but no good answer ever presented itself.

Collision with another vessel or with floating debris poses more of a threat than storms for small-boat sailors. Radar reflectors, consisting of small metal sheets formed into perpendicular planes and hung in the rigging, enhance a boat's chances of being picked up by a passing ship's radar, but they are not foolproof, and they pass the burden of collision avoidance to the oncoming vessel. Carl had given this matter plenty of thought, and he not only carried a top-quality reflector but also had an expensive radar unit aboard *La Vie en Rose*. The unit had a maximum range of 16 miles, allowing him to scan for ships beyond the visible horizon, and a range alarm alerted him whenever a ship or other target, including rocks and islands, penetrated a preset radius around the boat. Unfortunately, the radar didn't always work as advertised, and it consumed far too many precious amps of electrical power when transmitting.

Although *La Vie en Rose* was outfitted with a variety of ways to keep her vital 12-volt battery system charged, too many devices competed for her limited supply of power. Carl was usually forced to choose between running the autopilot and navigation lights or the radar, and the autopilot and lights always won. He would occasionally turn on the radar, especially at night, but rarely left it transmitting for long.

In the daylight it was easier to use his eyes, and Carl methodically scanned the horizon through 360 degrees. It was all clear. For the umpteenth time he ran the singlehanded sailor's familiar calculation: "We're doing 6 knots and a ship on a dead-on collision course is doing 20 knots. Assuming a distance to horizon of about 5 miles, we can't possibly get run down for at least 10 minutes." He glanced at his watch and dropped down into the seat behind the navigation desk. This simple time-speed-distance calculation was becoming more difficult to run through his weary brain every day.

Most singlehanded passages unfold in phases: After three days out you're exhausted. Six days out you find your stride, and nine days out you are once again exhausted, this time in your bones, and the passage seems as if it will never end. Retreating into the past is one way to keep your sanity—or disturb it, depending on what you run into there. Nine days at sea is enough time to replay your mind's entire hard drive for buried memories. While you might struggle to remember what course you plotted on the chart a few minutes before, staring out at the horizon you can reconstruct intimate details of Little League games. You remember girls you had crushes on and teachers you hated. You relive every high school date you had, every time love came your way or crushed you underfoot, every person you wronged, every cruel thing you said, every triumph and every humiliation you experienced. There is no escaping your thoughts on a small boat at sea. Your horizons are endless, but your borders are defined by the deck edge a few feet away. You're imprisoned in a tiny floating cell. In the right frame of mind it's a unique brand of freedom. In the wrong frame of mind it's torture. And always the demands of keeping boat and body together are relentless. Carl had discovered that blue-water passagemaking was much more challenging than the two-, three-, or even four-day hops he'd made along the coast the previous summer.

On the coffee-stained chart spread across the varnished teak surface of the nav table, he traced his last charted position. He'd plotted the coordinates, 22° 49′ north latitude and 64° 40′ west longitude, the evening before. As of the previous night, November 13, he was firmly in the tropics, now 40 miles or so south of the dashed line representing the Tropic of Cancer, but the weather didn't feel tropical. Carl was bundled up in a fleece sweater. Like many native Floridians, he was never able to adapt to cool weather, and even a modest drop in the mercury made him cold.

Closing in on the 22nd parallel, he knew there was nothing off his port side but ocean. The nearest land that way was Cape Blanc in the western Sahara, 3,000 miles away. To starboard, the Bahamas, the Turks and Caicos Islands, and Cuba all lay over the horizon, hundreds—not thousands—of miles to the west, but far enough to leave him feeling small and alone. East, east, east—that's the mantra for sailors departing the Atlantic coast of the United States for the Caribbean islands, and now Carl was east of the 65th meridian. A quick look at the GPS confirmed that he was still on track. His course was 190 degrees on the compass, which, after adjusting for magnetic variation, translated into 178 degrees on the chart—just a pinch left of due south.

Sailors must contend with shifting degrees of variation, an annoyance caused by the fact that the magnetic north pole—to which a compass points—does not coincide with the geographic north pole but wanders slowly through the high Canadian arctic. Only from a few select locations on earth will magnetic north happen to coincide with true north. Everywhere else, the degree and direction of local variation is indicated on charts and must be added to or subtracted from compass directions to get true courses. Although his GPS receiver automatically provided the compass course to the next waypoint, Carl always plotted his true course on the chart. It was the proper way to navigate.

Carl had marked his position the evening before, a small dot with a small circle around it, after talking to Ray Crawford, skipper of the nearby but unseen sailboat *MaRiah*. The two yachts had been communicating via single-sideband radio for several days. Crawford was Carl's lifeline to humankind. Not only was he a friendly voice on the radio, he was able to send e-mail messages back to Shelley Grund, Carl's former sister-in-law, who was maintaining his website from her home near Appleton, Wisconsin. It was like Carl to have retained his first ex-wife's sister as his best friend. It was also like Carl not to understand the technology involved in sending e-mails via SSB radio. He was content to rely on other sailors while at sea, and when he made port he would post up with Shelley from a harborside Internet café.

Crawford's latest e-mail to Shelley noted Carl's position and indicated that everything was "fine" aboard *La Vie en Rose*. He wrote that Carl expected to make landfall in a couple of days. "Sail on, Ragman," Crawford's message concluded. Carl had recently assumed this moniker for his e-mail and radio transmissions. He was enthralled by sailing, by the press of wind in the Dacron sails that drove *La Vie en Rose* across the sea. Sailing was for him far more than a method of travel; it was a communion with the sea, a manner of living, and a pact that accepted with equanimity the sea's joys and terrors. On his website Carl had given the definition of "ragman" as "one with a passion for life under sail." The name also merged his identity with a tradition of ocean wandering that stretched back to Ulysses. Carl had read all the books. Ragman was his Ishmael.

Carl had preprogrammed the National Weather Service weather channels into his SSB receiver, and now he flipped on the radio. He glanced at his watch. He still had 15 minutes before the High Seas forecast, and he was a few minutes overdue for a look around on deck. Back in the cockpit he scanned the horizon and punched a slight course change into the autopilot. There was no need to steer any extra miles. He was aiming directly for his waypoint, the light on Savana Island, 2 miles west of St. Thomas. The thought of the Virgin Islands so close at hand must have triggered bittersweet memories.

Carl had spent many happy days in the Virgins a decade before aboard his friend Tom Criste's 39-foot sloop. It was there, in those trade wind–cooled islands dented with perfect anchorages and speckled with beach bars, that Carl realized sailing might become something more than a hobby or a pleasant way to sustain a drinking habit. Crewing for a week or so at a time for Tom, his first civilian friend in twenty years, Carl not only had learned how to sail but also had sampled the cruising lifestyle, and he liked what he tasted. He encountered voyaging sailors from distant countries as they passed through the islands, and he came to believe that traveling the world by sailboat offered a means of escape, a way out of the mounting disenchantments that had bogged down his post-military life. The far horizon exerts a powerful pull on the disillusioned. Like many sailors before him, Carl imagined that one day he might cast off his troubles like a set of frayed docklines and sail into a new life.

Sadly, though Tom planted the seeds for Carl's dream, he failed to live long enough to see the dream become reality. He died a couple of months before Carl set off on his big passage. Carl had clung to the hope that somehow Tom would beat his cancer and join *La Vie en Rose* for a reunion cruise in the Virgin Islands. Carl cradled all his hopes longer than most. He kept closets full of boxed-up disappointments, boxes he was going through in those night hours on passage.

With the winds backing more into the northeast, Carl eased out the main- and jibsheets, the lines that controlled the working sails on his sleek double-headsail sloop. He sailed cautiously, using his smaller headsail unless the winds were very light, but he paid close attention to sail trim and kept his boat moving efficiently. He didn't want a sudden squall to catch him with too much sail flying, yet he knew that the faster he sailed, the sooner he'd eat a decent meal ashore and get a decent night's sleep. So he worked hard to make the most of a conservative sail set.

I can picture him sitting back, lighting a cigarette, inhaling deeply, and admiring the curve of each sail. He was a stickler for keeping the headsail's luff telltales—ribbons of fabric sewn into the sail's forward edge—streaming aft, an indication that the sail was trimmed for maximum efficiency. Sailboats are propelled not by catching wind but by bending it, and Carl loved to tell a captive audience how the wind curves around a foil, accelerating as it goes and developing lift. If he had paper at hand he would draw the vectors of lift and drag and heeling forces, showing their resolution into forward motion.

Most of all, he didn't want to overburden the autopilot. A working autopilot is essential for singlehanded sailing, and Carl did whatever he could to make his autopilot's job easier, even if it meant flying less sail than *La Vie en Rose* craved.

When it was time for the forecast, Carl went below, steeling himself. He knew he'd have to sit through nearly 30 minutes of Perfect Paul, the computer-synthesized voice the National Weather Service had adopted a couple of years before. Listening to the entire forecast was like listening to fingernails on a blackboard, but Carl always did so anyway. He tuned the SSB radio on 8 megahertz, searching for the best reception frequency. He had acquired radio ears and could shut out annoying static in order to decipher the important signals. Schoolteachers and parents possess similar skills. He tried 12 MHz before settling back on 8764 kilohertz, the forecast broadcast out of Chesapeake, Virginia. Paul, sounding like a robot from *Lost in Space*, droned on, describing the conditions for most of the western

Atlantic. In a dispassionate tone with the occasional odd empha-sis and mispronunciation, Paul noted gales and monster seas south of Iceland, brisk winds offshore from New England, and calms in the horse latitudes before finally reaching the tropical North Atlantic.

Carl took out his notepad. It was worth the wait. The fore-cast for his corner of the Atlantic called for light to moderate easterlies, the blessed trade winds, to build, and for generally fair weather to continue. Off to the southeast, a weak low-pressure system was stalled but was not likely to impact *La Vie*, at least not immediately. Paul was describing ideal sailing conditions for the next 24 hours for a small boat like *La Vie*. But Perfect Paul wasn't quite finished. He had a surprise.

The last part of the broadcast was the tropical weather out-look. Hurricane season was nearly over, and by mid-November tropical systems were rare in the Caribbean basin, or at least they used to be. Carl had delayed his passage until November precisely to limit the threat of encountering a tropical cyclone. Now Perfect Paul noted that a persistent low-pressure system in the far western Caribbean, which had been a weak tropical depression the day before, had become better organized. As of 1200 UTC (universal coordinated time, also known as Greenwich mean time, the time along the prime meridian pass-ing through Greenwich, England), which was equivalent to 0800 Atlantic Standard Time, *La Vie en Rose*'s local time, the system had been upgraded to a tropical storm, meaning that its sustained winds were over 34 knots. This new status called for a christening, and the storm was now named Lenny.

The name *Lenny* sounded more like a pimply-faced kid from Brooklyn than a brewing storm, but this Lenny was forecast to become a hurricane later in the day or, at the latest, by the next morning, November 15. Although Lenny was well west of *La Vie en Rose*, the news that the storm's future track was uncertain and that it was currently drifting eastward unsettled Carl. Having grown up in Florida, he knew a thing or two about hurricanes, and he'd never heard of one heading east. Wishing he'd paid more attention to the storm's exact coordinates, he reminded himself to be sure to listen to Herb Hilgenberg's weather net in the afternoon. Later, after lunch, he may have had a shot of Baileys to steady his nerves. He didn't need a hurricane to contend with, not on his first offshore passage. He'd weathered a few storms at anchor and a modest gale off the coast, but he wasn't prepared to test his heavy-weather sailing skills in a hurricane. He would have to do everything possible to avoid Lenny.

INTO THE EYE

"July, stand by
August, watch you must
September, remember
October, all over."

West Indian hurricane rhyme

In the early afternoon of November 14, the flight engineer and the dropsonde system operator finished their preflight inspections of the vintage WC-130 Hercules poised on the flight line at Homestead Air Force Base, south of Miami. Mules of the sky, these quixotic turboprop weather birds are capable of withstanding nature at its ugliest. Flying directly into the eye of a hurricane, a WC-130 takes measurements and deploys the GPS dropsondes that record and relay vital weather data back to the "customer," the forecasters at the National Hurricane Center in Miami.

The fleet of ten WC-130s was usually stationed at Keesler Air Force base in Biloxi, Mississippi, home of the Air Force Reserve's famed 53rd Weather Reconnaissance Squadron, the "Hurricane Hunters." The 1999 hurricane season had been busy, however, leading to the deployment of one Hurricane Hunter to MacDill Air Force Base in Tampa, Florida, where the National Oceanic and Atmospheric Administration usually maintained its fleet of three weather planes, and two others to Homestead.

Now the weather reconnaissance officer, Lieutenant Colonel Roy Deatherage, gave the thumbs-up from his seat on the flight deck, indicating that all the meteorological instruments were ready for action. Cleared for takeoff, the WC-130 was heavy with 60,000 pounds of fuel, enough for approximately 14 hours in the air. Every hour counts on meteorological missions, and the south Florida deployment trimmed an hour of flight time to most tropical hot spots. Taxiing onto the runway, the plane faced the prevailing easterly winds. With the deep engine roar that is a WC-130's signature, the converted cargo plane accelerated to a punchy 100 miles per hour. Designed for takeoffs and landings on the ragged dirt strips of shifting battlefields, the Hurricane Hunter needed less than half of the 10,000-foot runway to get airborne.

Gaining altitude, the vintage plane struck out over the Straits of Florida. Although bound south-southeast to investigate newly formed Tropical Storm Lenny, the navigator plotted an initial course to the south-southwest, toward the Yucatán Peninsula. The Hurricane Hunter would have to steer around Cabo San Antonio, the western tip of Cuba, before turning east to track down Lenny—which, according to the latest report, was meandering about 150 miles south of Kingston, Jamaica. Although the Air Force Reserve Hurricane Hunters work closely with NOAA, only NOAA planes had the authority in 1999 to fly through Cuban airspace. Civilian aircraft had been flying over Cuba for decades, but it seemed that acquiring critical data for predicting the future path of a hurricane, and in the process possibly saving hundreds or even thousands of lives with early warnings and timely evacuations, was not as important in 1999 as fighting old Cold War battles. Military planes would still be required to skirt Cuba in 2006.

The first reconnaissance flight two days earlier had had difficulty pinpointing the center of the poorly organized low-pressure system. Armed with satellite imagery, a second flight on November 13 had found a better-developed tropical depression, the sixteenth of the season. It was drifting slowly east, an unlikely track that was not expected to continue should the system develop into a more menacing threat. The crew of this third flight was aware that Lenny was now a tropical storm, strong enough to make entering the eyewall interesting, though not noteworthy.

In addition to the navigator and the flight engineer, the flight deck crew consisted of the aircraft commander in the left seat, the copilot opposite, and Lt. Col. Deatherage. WC–130s can carry a lot of cargo, human and otherwise, but the cargo compartment on a weather recon flight is almost empty. Only the dropsonde operator was riding in the back of the bus on this flight. There is nothing fancy about the accommodations in a Hurricane Hunter aircraft. The walls are bare metal, the seats are stiff and uncomfortable, and there are no flight attendants. And the ride can be rough. This is not a mission for anyone prone to motion sickness.

Eastbound at last, Deatherage noted that Lenny's anvil heads, with their jagged tops nearly 50,000 feet above the sea, made the storm easy to find in the otherwise clear skies of the western Caribbean. The clouds towered above the plane, which flew at 10,000 feet. One hundred miles from Lenny's poorly defined eye, Deatherage switched on the high-density data sensors that updated weather information every 30 seconds and relayed it to the National Hurricane Center. These measurements of temperature, humidity, barometric pressure, and altitude are the input parameters forecasters feed their computer models in their efforts to predict just what these swirling monsters might do. In addition, Deatherage gazed out the window and recorded his personal observations. Based on observed wave heights he estimated the winds at minimum hurricane strength, around 65 knots, and recorded the sea state at Force 12. The sea was confused, with whitecaps churning in several directions. It was no place to be in a boat, he thought to himself.

After the navigator picked up Lenny's eye more clearly on a special tilting radar, the crew prepared to enter the eyewall. Deatherage—who, in the summer of 2005, would be granted the "privilege" of flying into Category 5 Hurricane Wilma and recording the lowest barometric pressure ever, 883 millibars —was surprised by Lenny's strength, which the preflight briefing from the National Hurricane Center had not anticipated. Although he wasn't privy to all the information his computer was streaming back to the National Hurricane Center, it was clear that Lenny was intensifying despite the lateness of the season.

Entering the eye of a Category 1 hurricane may not be as exciting as penetrating a Category 5 storm, but it still commands attention. The plane was pelted with rain as powerful gusts caused it to buck in every direction. Hurricane Hunters concentrate on thunderstorm avoidance and weave their way into and out of storm cells. In Category 4 and 5 storms, rapid altitude losses of up to 1,000 feet are not uncommon. Sometimes things get even more exciting. Upon entering Hurricane Wilma in 2005, Deatherage and his crew would be caught in a downdraft that flattened their plane like a pancake, pushing it into a sudden vertical drop of more than 3,000 feet.

On November 14, however, the crew experienced only a minimal downdraft upon entering the newborn hurricane's eyewall. After a minute or so of turbulence, the WC-130 popped out on the other side into the calm eye of a tropical cyclone—a sight and sensation that, according to Deatherage, is eerie for the uninitiated. In the eye, which was just 15 to 20 miles across, the sky was a clear blue. But there was no time to tarry. The first GPS dropsonde, a 16-by-2¼-inch cylinder, was loaded into the launch tube. These 1-pound weather kamikazes contain sensors, a transmitter, and a battery bank. Once the first sonde was deployed, three more quickly followed.

Ten seconds after ejection, a tiny, square-coned chute popped open on each sonde, slowing its rate of fall to around 40 feet per second. Officially called dropwindsondes, these single-use instruments cost more than $500 each, and every other one fails to deliver the goods, sputtering silently into the sea. Still, when they do transmit, the information they provide is worth the price. Parachuting through the storm, a sonde is like a weather balloon in reverse. Like the sensors on the plane itself, the sonde measures wind speed and direction, air temperature, humidity, and barometric pressure while a preprogrammed GPS keeps track of its position as it descends. When dropped from around 10,000 feet, the sonde radios data back to the plane for roughly 3 minutes before it crashes and fizzles in the salty depths below. Like a suicide bomber, it gets one shot to do its job. Back on the flight deck, Deatherage and the dropsonde system operator edited the collected data and sent it off to the forecasters in Miami via SATCOM, the onboard satellite communication system. Though it took just a few seconds to deliver, the data would alter several lives forever.

The pilot steered back through the eyewall and out to a distance of about 100 miles to measure the extent of Lenny's wind field. This route formed the second leg of the X-shaped pattern that Hurricane Hunters typically fly, with each of the four legs of the X extending outward 100 miles. On the final pass into the eye, the plane's onboard sensors recorded 84-knot, or nearly 100-mile-per-hour, winds and a barometric pressure of 988 millibars, well below the normal sea-level pressure of 1012 millibars.

By the time the crew landed back at Homestead after an exhausting 11-hour mission, the Hurricane Center was ready to announce that Lenny had reached Category 2 on the Saffir-Simpson scale. This scale, developed by civil engineers Herbert Saffir and Bob Simpson in 1969, classifies hurricanes by sustained wind strength and by the damage they may inflict upon landfall. A Category 2 storm packs sustained winds from 83 to 95 knots and the potential to lift roofs, blow in windows, severely damage mobile homes and small craft, and flood low-lying coastal areas with a 6- to 8-foot storm surge. The Hurricane Center quickly posted hurricane warnings for Jamaica and the south coast of Haiti. A warning means that hurricane conditions are likely within 24 hours or less.

The official forecast called for the storm to continue drifting slowly eastward before eventually curving northeast, then north, and finally northwest.

But when would this turn take place?

A VOICE IN THE WIND

> "When the number of factors coming into play in a phenom-
> enological complex is too large, scientific method in most
> cases fails us. One need only think of the weather, in which
> case prediction even for a few days ahead is impossible."
>
> Albert Einstein, from an address at the Conference on
> Science, Philosophy and Religion, 1940

ROAD TOWN, the charming capital of the British
Virgin Islands, drapes around the inner harbor of Road Bay,
Tortola, like a pastel-colored shawl. In the fall of 1999, quaint
West Indian wood-frame buildings with corrugated tin roofs
and droopy porches were becoming harder to find among the
new concrete block structures designed to withstand the fury
of a hurricane and the ever-increasing storm surge of tourists.
The town was gearing up for the winter charter season, and an
armada of sailboats was being prepped for the arrival of sun-
starved baby boomers ready to spend a week or two tacking
around paradise, sailing from one cabana bar to the next.
Tortola is home to more charter sailboats per square foot of
waterfront than anywhere else in the tropics.

Back in the 1970s the British Virgin Islands embraced the
comparatively low-impact, environmentally friendly marine
recreation industry as an alternative to mass tourism, and it
has paid off handsomely. The islanders are prosperous and

haven't had to sell their souls to get there, a rare combination in the Caribbean. Although by the late 1990s Road Town hosted the occasional cruise ship, the BVIs had, for the most part, avoided selling out to cruise companies and the all-inclusive resorts that hoard tourist dollars and sequester visitors in fenced-off compounds.

Downtown Road Town was home base for the Caribbean Weather Center, a small private company providing detailed forecasts for radio weather nets and personal route planning services for sailors. Road Town is one of the few places on earth where an outfit like the Caribbean Weather Center could flourish. Sailing is the pulse of Tortola's economy, and in the highly competitive crewed charter business, many skippers consider a weather routing service a practical necessity—both a safety factor and a planning tool. If a skipper knew, for example, that an approaching front would produce cool north winds, he could route the charter to take advantage of the winds or at least minimize their impact on his guests.

On the afternoon of November 14, maverick forecaster and company founder David Jones saw a dangerous scenario brewing, but few were heeding his warnings. "I am not trying to say 'I told you so' to the National Hurricane Center," Jones said later, "but I felt like Lenny's west-to-east track was not only possible, but probable." Jones, who died in 2003, was something of a guru in the Caribbean, the author of *The Concise Guide to Caribbean Weather*, a bible for charter boat captains and cruisers. He sensed early on that Lenny meant trouble, not only for the Virgins but for all the Leeward Islands.

Jones explained later that a strong La Niña was forming in 1999. La Niña, the sister to El Niño, is a climatic condition characterized by cooler-than-normal water temperatures in the equatorial Pacific. What happens there doesn't stay there—it influences global weather. La Niña actually causes more havoc in the Caribbean than the better-known El Niño. Jones felt that La Nina was partially responsible for the extreme low pressure and large area of thundershowers that had lingered uncharacteristically in the western Caribbean for weeks on end before Lenny formed. During La Niña years, the Atlantic Basin experiences increased hurricane activity.

At the same time, farther north, a winter weather pattern was already taking hold, and stray cold fronts were meandering south to create strong west-to-east steering currents. A third factor was a low-pressure trough east of the Leewards that refused to budge and, in effect, was poised to draw Lenny east, Jones thought, "like a dog on a leash."

"Nobody wanted to hear what I had to say," Jones said, "at least not at first. Everybody assumed Lenny would eventually turn north. Our forecast models predicted the possibility of Lenny developing into a major hurricane. Maybe it was the uniqueness of the system, but insufficient heed was given to these warnings by some islands. Even here in the BVIs, we were too busy welcoming the end of storm season and getting our storm shutters down and our boats rigged to worry about a cyclone that was already south of Cuba. People thought it couldn't possibly affect the British Virgin Islands."

FINISH LINE AND STARTING POINT

"You must live in the present, launch yourself on every wave, find your eternity in each moment."

Henry David Thoreau, *Walden*

On the morning of November 14, 1999, Steve Rigby finished his breakfast at Le Pelican, a dockside café on the quay at La Marina de Rivière Sens, in Basse-Terre. He left 20 francs on the table, still wondering why the islanders had been slow to convert to the euro. Not a single frond rustled on the stately palm trees standing sentinel over the newest marina on Guadeloupe. Delicate orchids stood defiantly upright, unruffled by any trace of breeze. Steve could almost have cut the tropical air with the blunt lemon-peeling knife he had used to butter his baguette. It was miserably calm, especially for mid-November, when the trades would ordinarily have filled in. It was an ideal day for the topless French sunbathers already gathering on the beach, but not a good day for sailing—at least not yet.

Still, it is always hard to tell what the wind is really up to from the leeward side of a Caribbean island. For all Steve knew it might be blowing a gale on the windward side. He consoled himself with the knowledge that the wind was sure to come up later in the day, and that the bottled-up energy would eventually muster itself for a climb over the interior mountains. From there it would hurry down the backside as a gusty katabatic wind, creating a decent offshore breeze by late afternoon. And an offshore breeze was just what Steve needed. He'd be ready to sail by late afternoon.

The verdant, almost black volcanic spire of La Soufrière rose 4,800 feet above the sea, casting a morning shadow over a wide swath of Basse-Terre, or "low land." It was a sarcastic name for the high and rugged western half of butterfly-shaped Guadeloupe, the largest island between Puerto Rico and Trinidad. Walking back to the dock, Steve paused, once again struck by just how small his new boat was. It bobbed on the water like a teacup on a saucer, the wake from a puttering dinghy with a 4-horsepower outboard enough to send it rocking from side to side. At just over 21 feet it was little more than a toy, a souped-up go-cart of a sailboat, a sailing dinghy on steroids. It was hard to imagine that just two weeks earlier the boat had finished a grueling transatlantic race. It was smaller than the boats on which Steve had taught stockbrokers and lawyers how to sail in New York Harbor.

Steve had been on hand when the first Mini Transat boats crossed the line after racing across the Atlantic Ocean from the Canary Islands, but he almost hadn't made it to Guadeloupe. An Englishman turned Aussie, he was in the process of applying for U.S. citizenship, and the Immigration and Naturalization Service had been reluctant to allow him to leave the country before his paperwork came through. Just days before he had been scheduled to fly out, the INS had relented, and he had been among the three hundred or so spectators standing on the breakwalls near La Marina de Rivière Sens.

It was midnight, and they were cheering *Amor Lux*, the first boat home on the second leg. *Amor Lux* was sailed by Erwan

Tabarly, nephew of the late French sailing legend Eric Tabarly. *Voile Magazine*, skippered by French sailor Sébastien Magnen, limped home later the next day and, although under a jury rig, still managed to place first overall when the combined times for both legs of the race were tabulated. Steve had followed the race closely and was in touch with the father of one of the racers, negotiating to buy his son's boat when and if he finished.

The Mini Transat just may be the most challenging single-handed ocean race of them all. Other events, like the Vendée Globe and the Velux 5 Oceans, unfold over months as contestants sail larger, usually 50- to 60-foot boats around the world. The Mini Transat is an oceanic version of running with the bulls, except that the running goes on for two and a half to three weeks. Steve couldn't wait to become part of the next scheduled event in 2001.

Alex Bennett drove *English Braids* across the finish line just off the marina channel markers on November 1. The young Englishman was sixteen days and 4 hours out of Puerto Calero, Lanzarote, in the Canary Islands, finishing fifth overall. He was incredibly exhausted, thrilled at finishing well but disappointed at not doing even better. He had been in position to win when his autopilot, vital to singlehanded sailing, had failed. That had forced him to take down his sails whenever his mind and body demanded rest, allowing his closest competitors to pass him.

Steve Rigby helped Bennett secure his boat to the dock and was among the first to buy him a drink. Eventually Rigby told Bennett that he was buying his boat, and another toast was ordered all around. Young, talented Alex Bennett, a rising star in the sailing world, took to Steve right off. Few could resist his charms. Steve was well traveled, good-looking, and immensely likable. He was also on a mission, and Alex Bennett's boat was phase one.

Steve's new bride, Julia, an attorney in New York, wired the funds, virtually all of their savings, and they closed the deal a few days later. Bennett moved his gear off the boat, and after a week or so of showing Steve the ropes, flew back to England—but not before promising to help Steve prepare for the 2001 race. Steve was on his own, thrilled and nervous, for nothing is as telling as finally launching a long-nurtured dream. But Steve couldn't imagine failure. Everything was going right in his life, and he was intensely focused on the next step of his plan.

The immediate next step was to sail *English Braids* to an English-speaking island before he went mad. Guadeloupe was getting to him. He couldn't speak a word of French and understood even less. He also needed to remove his boat from French territory in order to avoid paying duties and taxes. Road Town, Tortola, a mere 225-mile hop to the northwest, was the logical destination. It was just far enough to serve as a good shakedown, but not so far as to warrant serious offshore preparations. And the locals there spoke English. Most important, he would be able to leave the boat under the watchful eye of his good friend and fellow sailing instructor Christian Pschorr, who was planning to spend the winter in the British Virgin Islands with his family aboard their small sloop. Steve planned to return frequently from his home in Manhattan to master the idiosyncrasies of the skittish Mini and garner as much time at the tiller as possible. The blustery Virgins would be an ideal test track. After a winter of bashing about the islands, he'd be ready for serious campaigning.

In the spring of 2000, Steve intended to ship the boat to

Europe and compete in the season's Mini events, further honing his skills for the big race, the next Mini Transat scheduled for 2001. If things went the way he hoped, the Mini campaign would be the prelude to something much bigger: it would be his launching pad into the high-stakes world of big-boat singlehanded sailing. Steve was dreaming about fame and fortune, about screaming down waves in a huge multihull in the Southern Ocean, about generous corporate sponsorships, about competing in storied singlehanded events like the Vendée Globe, the Around Alone, and others. Tiny *English Braids* was going to be his punch card into a most exclusive club.

Steve was late getting off the dock on November 14. As in the departure for every passage, there was one last item to check on the boat, one more part to buy, one more friend to visit, one more reason for delay. Alex Bennett had urged Rigby to get some sea time on the boat before shoving off for Tortola. Failing that, he suggested sailing in short hops and anchoring along the way, or at the very least rounding up a crew member. No chance. For all his charm Rigby was, according to his older brother Simon, genetically stubborn, and his mind was made up. He would sail to Tortola nonstop, and he'd sail alone. If he couldn't pull off a little hop like that, how was he ever going to race professionally?

He called Julia from the quayside phone and told her that the passage should take no more than 36 hours, but that she shouldn't start to worry unless she didn't hear from him for 48 hours. He assured her that he would sail safely and told her that he loved her. In a serious tone, he told her to call the Coast Guard if he didn't turn up on schedule. They had an emergency plan, and despite being thousands of miles away, Julia was the point person. Privately, though, Steve probably thought his

36-hour estimate was generous. He anticipated picking up the trades on the starboard quarter, popping his Mini's colorful spinnaker, and flying up to Road Town in 24 hours or less. Under the right conditions, Minis are rocket ships on water, and Steve was ready to see just what his new boat could do.

Simon Rigby is convinced that Steve was oblivious to the radio weather forecast, not because he wasn't interested but because the forecast was in French. He may have observed the weather chart posted in the marina office window, which clearly showed a deepening low to the west. In fact, the low was upgraded to a tropical storm as he prepared to sail, and would become a hurricane within hours of his departure. But even if he did check out the weather charts, they probably didn't concern him much. He knew that tropical systems in the Caribbean almost always move from east to west. The biggest weather worry in Steve's mind was a lack of wind, not too much of it, and besides, Tortola was only a couple of hundred miles away.

The afternoon was late by the time he cleared the break-walls and pointed his bow northwest. A Mini may be small, but it is a complex boat to sail. Only half as long as *La Vie en Rose* and weighing merely a twentieth as much, *English Braids* was much more challenging to handle. Not only did the sails need constant adjustment, but the mast itself, the twin rudders, and even the canting keel required fine-tuning. Steve no doubt had his hands full trying to decipher what line corresponded to what action as he coaxed *English Braids* along in exasperatingly light winds while the sun set. The situation was made more frustrating by the lack of a working autopilot. Steve had not taken the time to repair the instrument before sailing. He may not have noticed that there wasn't a trace of red in the sky, and that a layer of dark stratus clouds was building on the western horizon.

Or maybe he did. "Steve was always on the lookout for the green flash," Simon says. A sign of good luck, the green flash occurs immediately upon sunset when the horizon is clear. Just as the sun's upper limb drops below the horizon, a green ray of light appears. It's a rare event—most sailors are still looking for their first one—and nobody in the Caribbean witnessed one on the evening of November 14.

NOWHERE TO HIDE

"Between us there was, as I have already said somewhere, the bond of the sea."

Joseph Conrad, *Heart of Darkness*

Bobby's Marina occupies a thin, overcrowded strip of land between the new beach boardwalk and the cruise ship terminal on the northeast corner of Great Bay in Philipsburg, on the Dutch side of the binational island of St. Martin/Sint Maarten. It has been there forever—or at least since 1971, which is forever by Caribbean sailing standards. Back then, Bobby Velasquez drove the backhoe himself and coaxed a few jagged rocks into a modest breakwall to protect his burgeoning boatyard and marina. He begged and borrowed the money to install the railroad lift with which he hauled yachts out of the water the old-fashioned way, using a massive cable, a slow-turning winch, and a cradle mounted on steel rails. I hauled one of my old boats on Bobby's railroad lift in the late 1970s. The boat wobbled mightily as it lurched out of the water, like a seasick manatee. The railroad lift was woefully inefficient, and you had to work on your boat quickly so you didn't tie up space too long, but it was one of the few haulout facilities in the West Indies in those days.

Bobby later installed a mobile Travelift—perhaps the first in the Caribbean—which allowed him to haul more boats. He

plowed all his earnings back into the yard, continually expanding his facilities. He rebuilt after tropical storms and hurricanes, then expanded more. By the fall of 1999 Bobby's Marina
was known throughout the Caribbean as a yard where you
could get good work done at a fair price. Bobby didn't play
favorites: a beat-up fishing trawler, a 70-foot motor yacht, and
a 32-foot rough-and-ready cruising sailboat were not only shoe-
horned next to one another in the yard but treated equally.
Bobby, decked out in his trademark admiral's cap, was not one
to bask in success. He was more comfortable in the yard, discussing a repair project with a customer, than sitting in his
office. Not surprisingly, the yard was busy, and advance book-
ings were almost always required for a haulout.

On the afternoon of November 14, 1999, local charter boat
skipper Guillaume Llobregat, a regular customer at Bobby's,
came to a sudden conclusion. Far-off Tropical Storm Lenny,
drifting south of Jamaica and nearly 800 miles to the west, was
going to gather steam, become a hurricane, march across the
Caribbean from west to east, and smack St. Martin. While
many sailors based on the island were taking a more wait-and-
see attitude, doubting that Lenny would follow this unprecedented track, Llobregat convinced himself that the storm was
coming his way. He was an experienced sailor, and like mete-
orologist David Jones he apparently saw that there was nothing in the atmosphere to turn the storm around. Although just
36 years old, Llobregat was a longtime resident of St. Martin,
and he shared with many other Caribbean charter skippers an
innate sense about tropical storms. He feared and loathed
them and would go to almost any lengths to keep his boat safe.

Hurricane Luis, which had walloped St. Martin four years
earlier with 115-knot winds, had proved that the only place a

boat was safe during a major hurricane was securely propped up on hard ground in a boatyard. Llobregat knew that it was the storm surge that damaged boats, not high winds. When Hurricane Jose had strafed St. Martin just a month before, Llobregat and his *Frederic-Anne* had ridden out the storm without incident while hauled out at Bobby's Marina. He had every intention of weathering Lenny in similar fashion.

Frederic-Anne was a handsome 65-foot ferrocement schooner, built professionally in Brittany. With ample deck space and a classic rig, commercially certified to carry up to twenty-five passengers, she was well suited for day chartering. Many ferrocement boats are homebuilt monstrosities of crumbling concrete and exposed and rusting reinforcing bar and wire mesh, the handiwork of sailing dreamers who would have been better off as insomniacs. Ferrocement lends itself to amateur construction but not often to good amateur construction. Boatbuilding should be left to professionals, and *Frederic-Anne* was one of the few well-built ferrocement boats. She was Llobregat's pride and joy as well as his means of support. Together with his wife, Alicia, he worked the boat hard, running day charters out of Marigot, on the French side of St. Martin. The powerful, black-hulled sailing yacht was well known to all the local tour hucksters and did a thriving business ferrying day-trippers to the azure waters of nearby Anguilla and conducting sunset cruises in Marigot harbor.

Llobregat maintained the boat in good condition and had given her a complete refit at Bobby's Marina earlier in the summer. The rigging, sails, and engine had all been upgraded. She was shipshape and ready for the season just getting underway in mid-November. *Frederic-Anne* had been back in the water only three weeks, and her fresh paint still shimmered. Ever prudent, Llobregat had delayed launching the boat until after Hurricane Jose passed. Now, although already in the hole after paying Bobby for the refit, Llobregat didn't want to take any chances with Lenny. Hauling would be an expensive hassle, but he made the decision to sail back over to Bobby's. Once all danger from Lenny was past, he'd relaunch to begin what he anticipated would be a busy charter season.

On the quay at Marina Royale, Marigot's lovely inner harbor, Llobregat downed an espresso and hit the docks. It didn't take him long to find local sailor Jacques Santos, his steady mate, who quickly agreed to help him deliver *Frederic-Anne* to Bobby's. Santos, a Brazilian, had been based in St. Martin for a couple of years and made his living crewing on charter boats. For most of that time he'd been regular crew aboard *Frederic-Anne* and considered the skipper a friend. He was 26 years old and an enthusiastic sailor, although he lacked offshore experience.

Llobregat and Santos hauled up *Frederic-Anne*'s hefty anchor and headed west around the Lowlands, a lovely residential area west of Marigot. On a prominent hill in this misleadingly named district, Llobregat could see his family compound, with its commanding view of the sea. Schooners can be cumbersome to sail with just two people, and Llobregat didn't hesitate to fire up the big six-cylinder diesel. This wasn't a charter, and they were in a hurry. They made their way south and then east along the coast to Philipsburg. Motoring up into Great Bay, Llobregat noticed a whirlwind of activity near Bobby's. The marina and boatyard were jammed with boats, and several other vessels were circling near the haulout slip, each hoping to be lifted next. Llobregat was not the only sailor worried about distant Tropical Storm Lenny.

Contacting Bobby on the VHF radio, Llobregat learned that

the yard was full. "My hands were tied," Bobby said later. "There was no space available. I had nowhere to put the boat. I had to put my own barges in the water to make space. He got here too late."

Llobregat, a kind-hearted if not openly warm man, was polite. He understood that Bobby was terribly busy. He offered to anchor out in the bay and wait until the lift was free, but Bobby said there was simply no room. Llobregat then turned to pleading, insisting that he had an agreement with Bobby to haul the boat when a storm threatened. Bobby stonewalled. Llobregat became more insistent, then angry. He was a good customer, he said, and had just spent a tidy sum with Bobby. He was furious that Bobby refused to haul *Frederic-Anne*. When he at last reluctantly accepted that he would not be accommodated, he spun the wheel over and steamed defiantly out of the harbor.

At this point he made a curious and fateful decision. If he couldn't find safe haven ashore, he'd sail out of harm's way. He would be proactive. He was not going to crowd into Simpson Bay Lagoon, one of the Caribbean's most overrated hurricane holes, and pray that Lenny veered away from the island. He would do his own veering. Besides, he had already loaned his secure 3-ton mooring to a friend, and he had nowhere to go in the lagoon. He and Santos sailed back to Marigot and anchored in the harbor. Llobregat told Santos to meet him early the next morning. They would take *Frederic-Anne* to sea. They would monitor Lenny's position on the radio and return when the coast was clear. To hell with Bobby.

HAVANA

> "In a museum in Havana there are two skulls of Christopher Columbus, one when he was a boy and one when he was a man."
>
> Mark Twain, *The Adventures of Thomas Jefferson Snodgrass*

It is only a 35-minute flight from Montego Bay, Jamaica, to Havana's José Martí International Airport, but after 4 hours I still had not cleared customs. Welcome to Fidel's fiefdom. It was November 14, 1999, and I had come to Cuba for two reasons. First, I had an assignment to interview and write a magazine piece about Gregorio Fuentes, who had been Ernest Hemingway's captain, friend, and confidant. Now 102, at age 100 Fuentes had become something of a celebrity. He was one of the few living links to Papa and the last one trying to cash in on the writer's enduring fame. When my writing work was complete, I would shift into sailing mode and make preparations to sail a friend's 49-foot sloop from Havana to St. Thomas.

I hoped to complete both tasks promptly and get underway in a day or two. I anticipated a tough week's passage down the Old Bahama Channel, the sliver of deep water between the shallow banks of the southern Bahamas and Cuba's reef-fringed northern coast. I had plans to rendezvous with my friend Carl Wake for Thanksgiving dinner in St. Thomas. I couldn't wait to hear about his passage. But first I had to clear customs.

My journalistic credentials failed to impress the stern-faced agents. They were convinced I was up to no good because I was carrying a handheld VHF radio and a GPS receiver in my luggage. I was traveling with Bill Williamson, a retired Brazilian journalist and sailing pal, who, speaking fluent Spanish, finally convinced them that I would not be snooping around the island and radioing strategic coordinates to the CIA. Havana was hosting a summit meeting of Latin American leaders, and Castro wasn't taking any chances. Security was tight. Eventually we made it through the airport and found our way to the boat.

No sooner had we tossed our bags aboard than a TV news crew from Miami pounced on us, bombarding me with questions. "Are you an American?" "How were you able to travel to the island?" "Is this your boat?" "What do you think about Castro hosting this summit?" The last thing I wanted to do after the customs ordeal was to draw attention to myself. I politely deflected the questions and hurried down the dock into the marina bar, needing a mojito.

Cuba is just like the rest of the world in that a TV blares in every bar. This one was tuned to the Weather Channel, and although the picture was grainy I recognized the ominous music preceding a tropical storm update. Good timing, I thought to myself. White-haired hurricane expert John Hope soon appeared, looking concerned and a little confused. Hope explained that a Hurricane Hunter aircraft had just returned from investigating Tropical Storm Lenny. Lenny was strengthening and was expected to become a hurricane that night, making it the eighth of the busy 1999 season. At first I wasn't worried. Lenny was well south of Cuba and seemed unlikely to affect our upcoming passage along the northern coast.

Then the Weather Channel displayed the forecast track. The

yellow cone showed Lenny drifting slowly east then northeast toward Hispaniola in the next few days. After that the cone flared dramatically. Exactly where Lenny was headed was anybody's guess. John Hope seemed to think that it would eventually turn north. This was a wrinkle I didn't need. It began to look as if I might be spending a few more days than planned in Havana. Of course, there are worse places to be stranded.

I wondered where Carl was. He had to be getting close to St. Thomas.

LA VIE EN ROSE

"Hold me close and hold me fast
  The magic spell you cast
  This is la vie en rose.
  When you kiss me heaven sighs
  And tho I close my eyes
  I see la vie en rose."

Louis Armstrong's version of "La Vie en Rose"

A GRAY sky overtopped darker gray stratus clouds. Gray waves rolled ashore under gray, driven snow. Gray seagulls circled over the gray, weather-beaten boardwalk, piers, and hotels. The haggard faces of the all-night gamblers were gray. Even the inherent optimism of a boat show couldn't cheer Atlantic City in February 1996. Stranded on cradles, the boats on display seemed out of place in the cavernous gray convention center. Bright banners hung limp in the frosty air. Charter companies flaunted posters of beautiful people sprawled on shimmering decks off tropical islands, but the posters were more jarring than alluring, ripe for ridicule from the crowd of cynical keel kickers with their Jersey accents.

It was a tough crowd, a local crowd, a walkup crowd. For the most part they were the only ones who could get to the show, because a winter storm had blanketed the Middle Atlantic coast. The promoters should have bottled the warm trade winds from the Miami show the week before and let them waft across the drafty hall. Even the few serious sailors milling around the boats and display booths were scowling like the forlorn folks in the casino next door.

I was giving a talk on "How to Choose a Boat for World Cruising," one of dozens of seminars scattered around the perimeter of the ancient hall. "Remember," I said in conclusion, "a boat is only the vehicle to fulfill your dreams. Don't wait until you can afford the ultimate boat. It may be too late. Find a boat and go cruising now. It may be new, it may be used, it may be big or small. It doesn't matter. When the cruise is over you never talk about the boat anyway; it's the places and your experiences that you remember. Time is your most precious asset. It's the one thing you can't replace."

The crowd of eight to ten people clapped politely and hastily filed out of the room. I collected my notes, took a swig of water, and wondered what I was doing in Atlantic City. It had seemed like a good idea to come north to flog a few books and sign up customers for workshops and training cruises, but as the week dragged on and I found myself saying the same things over again, I longed to be back on my boat in Ft. Lauderdale, finishing preparations for an upcoming cruise to Central America. I needed to heed my own advice.

A lean, sandy-haired man lingered until the room was empty.

"Hi John," he said, in a deep drawl that had no sharp edges. "My name is Carl Wake. I really enjoyed your talk. You make a lot of sense."

We shook hands.

"I don't want to intrude on your busy schedule, but if you have a little time I'd sure love to buy you a cup of coffee and pick your brain." His silky Southern charm made it impossible to say no. My schedule wasn't that busy, and since I am no gambler there was little else to do in Atlantic City in February. The night before, I'd thrown snowballs at seagulls from the pier and wondered why they hadn't flown south.

We made our way to the snack bar, ordered coffee and bratwursts, and found a table. When Carl began to tell his story, I could have finished each sentence. I'd heard it before, from countless dreamers encountered at boat shows and on barstools. He was ready to change his life, to sail the world. He was in the market for a cruising boat, but even the most inspired dreams clash with reality eventually—or at least with financial reality. "I'd love to buy a new boat—I really like that new Island Packet down on the floor—but I can't afford it," he said sheepishly, as if not having an obscene amount of surplus cash to drop into a new boat meant that he had flunked the American Dream and become a washed-up relic. "So, I'm looking at secondhand boats, but where do I start?" The sheer variety of used boats left him bewildered.

His sailing experience was limited, but something about Carl's plans and his manner spoke to me directly: the way his almond eyes lit up when he mentioned distant landfalls he hoped to make, the way his warm smile failed to mask the urgency in his voice, the way he fully expected his future travels to be filled with as many tribulations as perfect sunsets. His dreams, like most sailing dreams, had been spawned and nurtured between the covers of nautical books and glossy magazines. "Look," he continued, with his palms turned out and an expression somewhere between a scowl and a grin, "I've read a lot of books. You name it, I've read it. Practical stuff like the Pardeys, Roth, and Dashew. Cruising stories—Slocum, Moitessier—they're all on my shelf. And classics too: Conrad,

Melville, Patrick O'Brian. I just can't get enough of the sea. But I'm tired of reading. Now I am ready to write my own story."

I ordered more coffee and studied the man sitting across from me. He was a tad less than 6 feet tall and weighed around 170 pounds. He was trim and in good shape, but obviously not a workout fanatic. From the radiating spider lines around his eyes, I guessed that he looked younger than he was. He had an odd but amusing way of conducting a conversation in spurts that were punctuated by long pauses as he gathered his thoughts. He was polite almost to a fault, and outwardly self-deprecating, but it was plain that his plans had been incubating a long time. He had every intention of pursuing them, regardless of what I or anyone else thought, yet he made me feel that my contributions to the conversation were essential.

"I want a boat I won't outgrow," he said, "and a boat that's big enough to carry my wife and me comfortably. I plan to start along the coast of Florida and in the Caribbean, but then I want to stretch my wings. I want to head up to Alaska and then out to the South Pacific. Those canals off Patagonia look mighty interesting too. The point is, I don't want to be restricted by latitude."

Here was a man who had never spent more than a few days at sea telling me that he planned to point the bow of an as-yet-unknown boat toward some of the planet's most dangerous waters. And the measure of his conviction was that I believed he would do just that. Leaning back in his chair, he smiled. "But I am not a wealthy man, and as you can see, I am not a young man. I can't afford to buy the wrong boat. That's where you come in."

Coffee turned to beer, and we burned a hole in the gray afternoon talking boats and getting to know each other. I learned that he was from Bradenton, on the west coast of Florida, and had grown up running motorboats around the shifty sandbars of the Manatee River. At least he knew that tides rise and fall and that salt water needs to be respected. He had done a bit of sailing with a friend in the Virgin Islands and had chartered on his own off the coast of Florida. He'd helped another friend on some coastal deliveries and had completed a liveaboard cruising course. He was farther down the nautical path than many of the would-be voyagers I encountered as an "expert," a purveyor of blue-water wit and wisdom.

Carl told me he had attended West Point, had been stationed all over the world, and had left the army after twenty years. He had settled in Atlanta, where he was renovating a house with his second wife. It was the thinnest outline of a life, but the things left unsaid, the pauses and the pursed lips, suggested that the hurdles of finding and affording a boat were not going to be the most difficult ones for Carl to clear. I wondered to what extent his wife shared his dreams.

Like everyone meeting Carl for the first time, I liked him instantly. Before we parted, I suggested that he come down to Ft. Lauderdale and attend a boat-buying workshop I was conducting later in the year. He didn't need much convincing. It was just what he was looking for.

The workshops had several purposes. They allowed aspiring cruisers to poke into every nook and cranny of several different boats without a yacht broker peering over their shoulders. They provided a forum for direct questions and straight answers, not something yacht brokers are known for. And they offered me a way to a make a little money while keeping close to home and my two young daughters. For years I had made landfalls for a living, delivering sailboats all over the world. The pay was moderate at best, and the working conditions occasionally hazardous, but I loved the work. Between deliveries I had put together modest expeditions that resulted in books and magazine articles. Sailing and writing, I'd managed to make it through twenty-plus years of adulthood without holding down a "real" job.

When Carl joined a handful of other dreamers for two days of sailboat immersion, we examined a variety of offshore boats ranging from a sleek Contessa 32 to a roomy Hylas 44. I did my best to dispel his romantic notions. He liked heavy, long-keeled boats with sweeping sheerlines and traditional bowsprits, the kind of boat that makes you think of Tahiti when you're hunkered in an armchair during a winter storm in Des Moines. Unfortunately, many traditional boats are slow, cumbersome, and not as seaworthy as they look. I extolled the virtues of a nimble hull shape with a fin keel and a skeg-hung rudder. A fin is a partial keel—think of a shark swimming upside down—and a skeg is an underwater protuberance behind the keel, like an airplane's tailfin, that supports and protects the rudder. I told Carl that if he and his wife were really going to sail shorthanded across the oceans of the world, he needed an easy-to-handle sail plan and an easily driven hull, not a floating bathtub and a false sense of security.

I offered the winsome Contessa 32, a small sloop that I had sailed around Cape Horn fifteen years before, as an example of a capable hull shape. "This is a great sea boat," I told Carl, with the fervor of a missionary converting the heathen, and I meant it. The low-slung Contessa has an almost perfect hull shape, one that never takes a punch but slices through the waves instead of pounding into them. Its soft motion in a seaway is not something to underestimate. A boat that pounds beats up its crew, and a beaten-up crew will make mistakes at sea. A boat doesn't nccd massive bronze fittings to be seaworthy. The Contessa weighs less than 10,000 pounds but is capable of sailing anywhere. Its only drawback is its small and miserable interior, with barely room enough to stand up in the main cabin, making it impossible to live aboard with any grace. I told Carl that what he needed was a bigger version of a boat like the Contessa 32.

The evening after the workshop concluded, I invited Carl to see my steel ketch *Fortuna*, which was also my home. He turned up with a bottle of Baileys, but I stayed with Bombay Sapphire. While my daughters played with Carl's golden retriever, Bijou, on the dock, amazed at his endless desire to chase and destroy tennis balls, Carl and I chatted long into the night. Carl was curious about steel boats until I pointed out the corrosion blossoming all over mine. Quoting the Neil Young album, *Rust Never Sleeps*, I said, "You don't want a steel boat for a first boat, especially a used steel boat. They require too much maintenance. You want to spend your time sailing, not chipping and painting."

Our conversation turned from boats to world cruising routes, and we talked of landfalls we hoped to make. I was intrigued with the undeveloped coasts of Central America and longed to get back to the Mediterranean. Carl wanted to explore the Inside Passage of the Pacific Northwest to Alaska. Finally, well primed by booze, we wandered into the subject of personal freedom, the true catalyst for these dreams.

Carl's concept of freedom had come to be embodied by a mariner in a storm, wholly responsible for himself, accountable to no one else, asking no quarter from thc sca, mcasuring his worth by his immediate actions. He had nurtured this vision with the books of Miles Smeeton, Vito Dumas, and Bernard Moitessier. Moitessier, the best-known sailor of the postwar generation, rejected the pleasures of society for a hard, simple life at sea, plying the oceans in his 39-foot steel ketch *Joshua*. In his international bestseller *The Long Way*, he wrote:

> *I am a citizen of the most beautiful nation on earth.*
> *A nation whose laws are harsh yet simple, a nation that*
> *never cheats, which is immense and without borders,*
> *where life is lived in the present. In this limitless nation,*
> *this nation of wind, light and peace, there is no other*
> *ruler besides the sea.*

Of course, Moitessier's embrace of the sea was not as uncomplicated as he made it out to be. He is best known for abandoning the first nonstop singlehanded around-the-world race in 1968, even though his eventual victory was virtually assured. As tellingly chronicled in Peter Nichols's book *A Voyage for Madmen*, when Moitessier chose to continue sailing east after rounding Cape Horn, instead of turning north to Europe and home, he did so without consulting his wife or children and without regard for anyone or anything but his own convictions. When he finally passed word to his family and the press, he wrote:

> *My intention is to continue the voyage, still nonstop,*
> *toward the Pacific Islands, where there is plenty of sun*
> *and more peace than in Europe. Please do not think that*
> *I am trying to break a record. 'Record' is a stupid word*
> *at sea. I am continuing nonstop because I am happy at*
> *sea, and perhaps because I want to save my soul.*

Moitessier never reconciled his need for solitude with his abandoned family. He wrote in his log, "I am fed up with false gods, always lying in wait, spiderlike, eating our liver, sucking our marrow." He could not stomach arriving to fanfare in Europe, yet *The Long Way* reached a huge audience, including Carl Wake, who had devoured all of Moitessier's books.

Miles Smeeton, quoting his indomitable wife, Beryl, in his classic 1959 sea story *Once Is Enough*, echoed Moitessier's sentiments. The Smeetons were thirty-five days at sea, in the Southern Ocean, zeroing in on Cape Horn, when Miles called the sea cruel. His wife took exception:

> *'Not the cruel sea,' Beryl said. 'The sea is impersonal. I don't see how you can call it cruel. It's the people on it who are apt to be cruel. I don't think you would call mountains or the sea cruel. It's only that we are so small and ineffective against them, and when things go wrong we start blaming them and calling them cruel.'*

Shortly after the Smeetons and their crew member and good friend John Guzzwell concluded this discussion, their boat was pitchpoled in a monstrous gale. Miraculously they survived the encounter, jury-rigged their beloved ketch *Tzu Hang*, and limped into a Chilean port. They never blamed the ocean, God, or anything else for sending a massive rogue wave their way, accepting it instead as part of the sailor's pact. Their sea was not cruel. The Smeetons continued to make voyages, including a successful rounding of the Horn, until late in life.

Vito Dumas, one of the greatest solo sailors of all time, broke the "chains of the treadmill of today and tomorrow" in 1942 and made an epic circumnavigation via the world's five great southern capes—the Cape of Good Hope; Cape Leeuwin, marking the southwest point of Australia; Tasmania's South East Cape; South West Cape on New Zealand's South Island; and, of course, legendary Cape Horn, perched at the foot of South America.

Dumas endured incredible hardships aboard his 31-foot ketch, but to him there was no alternative. He could not accept the madness of a world plunged into terrible war, nor did he want to be a cog in the industrial machinery and social upheaval that was transforming his native Argentina. The Southern Ocean, wild and treacherous as it was, offered sanity in an otherwise insane world.

These and other bold but disillusioned voyagers, searching for adventure and their souls after the madness of two world wars, have been called collectively the Ulysses Generation, and in their larger-than-life brushes with annihilation in pursuit of freedom, Carl Wake—West Point graduate and army colonel—recognized a deeply inviting and congenial kinship. He longed to join this quixotic club.

Two dreamers with two bottles make a dangerous mixture. At least we were securely moored to the dock, though at one point in the evening, as the breeze rustled the trees, we did talk about casting off and setting sail. Fortunately that idea was forgotten as I poured another round. It's highly unlikely that in our state we could have negotiated the six bridges spanning the narrow, snaking New River to reach open water. We turned to literature instead.

Carl's favorite book, at least his favorite that night, was *Islandia*, a classic utopian novel by Austin Tappan Wright. Written in the 1920s, the book describes an island off the coast of South America where people live in blissful isolation. The simple agrarian society is neat and orderly. Materialism is scorned. The islanders, a select group, have all sought out this stress-free paradise. They are free of needs and therefore of wants. Islandia was the destination of Carl's dreams, the metaphorical landfall he hoped to make after he had proven himself worthy.

Carl went home the next day nursing a hangover and a renewed vigor to sell the farmhouse he'd been restoring for more than five years. The equity in the house would translate into a good boat—or at least that was the plan. He had pushed the fast-forward button on his dreams. Instead of waiting two more years, the financially responsible choice, he had decided to start looking for a boat immediately.

He knew that changes loomed on his personal horizon. His wife had plans of her own, and sailing the high seas with Carl was no longer at the top of her list. Indeed, it wasn't on her list at all.

CARL had met Beatrice Loubatier in Atlanta in the late 1980s. Tall with strawberry-blonde hair, young, beautiful, and half-French, she enchanted Carl. After a decade of prowling the bars of Buckhead, the trendy nightclub district north of Atlanta, making one conquest after another, he was smitten with Bea from the beginning. Seeing in her the next great love of his life, he convinced himself that he was finally ready to settle down again. They had a whirlwind affair. Bea longed for excitement, and Carl had exciting dreams. They made a perfect match—perfect, that is, until Carl tried to stir his slow, simmering dreams into the same pot with her fast-moving day-to-day reality. Carl proposed on Valentine's Day, 1988, on a beach in Cancún under a full moon. By the time I met Carl in 1996, his dreams were still cooking and the marriage was already in the freezer.

Soon after their honeymoon, which they spent sailing with Carl's friend Tom Criste in the British Virgin Islands, they drew up a master plan. After buying an old farmhouse in Ellenwood, near Atlanta, they would spend three or four years refurbishing it. Then they'd sell it and buy a cruising boat with the profits. Carl, who had left the military after suffering a heart attack and undergoing subsequent bypass surgery, drew a hefty pension that would keep them cruising in style once they purchased the boat. In the meantime, he would need to become a competent skipper and Bea would need to learn to sail, a couple of minor details in their grand plan. They enrolled in a weeklong sailing course in Bradenton, Florida, right across the river from where Carl's mother lived.

The course was taught on a 35-foot cutter by a crusty, retired Orlando SWAT team cop. Carl described the skipper as "uptight, antisocial, and undiplomatic," adding, "we hit it off well!" Carl enjoyed the week immensely, learning to trim sails, set an anchor, and navigate. They even spent a night at sea. Unfortunately, Bea was miserable. She was seasick most of the time and uncomfortable being cooped up with strangers on a small boat. Carl later wrote that this well-intentioned but ill-fated week was when their "life plan" began to crumble.

Their next step was to charter a 29-foot Island Packet cutter for a week of puttering about Tampa Bay. The seas were smooth and Bea wasn't seasick. Carl gained confidence as a skipper, docking a "big" boat for the first time, and Bea enjoyed the privacy. Still, something was missing. Sailing just wasn't much of a turn-on for Bea. It seemed like a lot of work, and if she was going to work that hard she might as well get paid for it. Their concepts of cruising clashed. While Carl anticipated challenging days at sea, Bea had visions of sunbathing on the deck. Carl continued to sail when he could, accompanying his former instructor on short deliveries, but it became more difficult to convince Bea to spend time on the water.

Bea's life was changing. She had left her job as a secretary and become a flight attendant for Delta Airlines. Now she traveled a lot, and she and Carl were drifting apart. Only half in jest, Carl wrote to me that he had a unique talent for giving beautiful young women the financial and emotional support to start challenging new careers that they then found more interesting than him. A few weeks after the workshop in Ft. Lauderdale, he was talking about the need to find a boat he could sail alone. He wasn't quite ready to quit on Bea, telling me that their new plan was for her to fly in and join him when he arrived in a new port. She'd spend a few days, then return to work. But I knew this was just a preliminary step toward separation, part of the unmating dance, and so did Carl.

The next year was extremely difficult for Carl. His marriage was quietly collapsing, and his mother died. His house wouldn't sell, and his master plan had not only been seriously amended but was thoroughly bogged down. We corresponded often, and he made a few trips to Ft. Lauderdale to look at boats, but he felt guilty wasting my time. I enjoyed his company, but Carl's unhurried Southern mannerisms could test anyone's patience. At times I blew him off, but Carl never bristled. He knew that I was a good if unreliable friend. Carl understood my quirks and accepted them. When we did talk, I listened to his ever-evolving plans.

Finally the house sold. "Good God Almighty, I am free at last," he e-mailed, announcing that he was headed to Ft. Lauderdale. He piled Bijou into his old van and headed south in November 1997. It was time to stop talking, time to find a boat. We had struck a deal. I would be his adviser—not his broker, since I wasn't licensed to sell boats and didn't want to sell them. I used my connections with brokers to let us look at boats on our own. After taking less for the house than he had originally wanted and working out a settlement with Bea,

Carl's boat budget was down to $100,000, but that was still plenty of money to buy an offshore cruising sailboat. We went to work, poring over listing sheets.

Carl felt that 40 feet was the biggest boat he could handle safely by himself. I told him that length was less important than design. We looked at a lot of boats, including a Valiant 40, a well-respected design with many circumnavigations to its credit. It was cheap because its hull was peppered with fiberglass blisters. Carl liked a rugged Shannon 38 pilothouse sloop, but it was too expensive. We inspected a handsome Caliber 38, a well-cared-for Bristol 40, and a tired but still expensive Pacific Seacraft 37. All of these boats were capable cruisers, but none was quite right for Carl. He grew anxious, while I advised patience. The ideal boat would turn up if we kept looking.

I knew that *Soleil* was perfect for Carl the moment I stepped aboard in February 1998. A friend, yacht broker Rob Jordan, had insisted we look at the boat. A 42-foot double-headsail sloop, the boat had just arrived in town. Designed by Angelo Lavranos, South Africa's premier naval architect, *Soleil* had been built near Johannesburg in 1994, and no one would ever have guessed that she'd recently made the long crossing from South Africa. She was in terrific condition and well equipped for blue-water sailing.

Carl was intrigued but wary. We'd stumbled onto a boat that was not on the short list of coveted designs he'd developed from his years of research. *Soleil* was a classic "through the cracks" boat, an oceangoing thoroughbred that few Americans would place a checkmark next to on a one-line listing in the back of a sailing magazine. Low slung and well built, *Soleil* had a powerful fin keel, a skeg-hung rudder, and an easy-to-handle sail plan. The boat even had a narrow, molded-in swim step on the stern, a key feature for manhandling 85-pound Bijou from the dinghy to the deck. I had not been able to convince Carl to leave the drooling monster with Bea. Bijou was going cruising too.

Carl stood perplexed, muttering, "Um, well, um, I really like this boat but I don't know anything about it." I explained that Lavranos was a well-known designer who had worked for Sparkman and Stephens, preeminent American yacht designers, before returning home to open his own office. I also told him about other South African boats I knew of, including my brother-in-law Trevor Richards's *Wandering Star*, a 37-foot cutter he had sailed around the world. "South African boats are usually not finished in the yacht-like way we're accustomed to," I said, "but they are strong and seaworthy. They have to be. It blows like hell down around the Cape of Good Hope." There were plenty of South African boats on the market all along the East Coast; a sailboat was one way to smuggle money out of that rapidly changing country.

On a cocktail napkin over lunch, we scribbled the boat's pros and cons. The pros took an overwhelming lead, spilling onto a second napkin, while the only con was a lack of resale value for a boat nobody had heard of. "But I am not planning on selling, so that's not much of a con," Carl said. He studied the line drawings on the listing sheet. "You know, John, this boat looks like a bigger version of the Contessa 32, doesn't it? They're asking $120,000. Do you think I can get it for $100,000?" I nodded and laughed. I knew Carl had found his boat. Now it was just a matter of massaging the deal.

Carl offered $90,000. The sellers, a young couple who had returned to South Africa after sailing across the Atlantic, countered at $110,000. Carl upped his ante, and they countered again before an agreement was reached. The final price was $100,000, subject to survey and sea trial. Rob Jordan convinced the owners to let me conduct the sea trial.

Carl tossed the lines ashore and I maneuvered out of the crowded canal. We made our way down the river and into the commercial turning basin at Port Everglades. Carl was impressed by the way the sleek hull punched through power-boat wakes without a hint of pounding. Clear of the break-waters, we raised the sails—or unfurled them, to be precise. They were crisp, full of life, and extremely easy to deploy from the cockpit. Even the mainsail was controlled with an in-the-mast roller-furling system. At first Carl was skeptical of this arrangement, but after rolling it in and out several times, he saw the obvious advantages. He would be able to set and furl any sail without leaving the cockpit, a considerable safety feature. The boat was designed for singlehanded sailing.

We sailed back into the port and made our way to the boat-yard where we had scheduled a haulout to inspect the hull, keel, and rudder. Surveyor Paul Anstey met us at the yard. Anstey climbed through the boat, making notes and checking items on his survey form. With the boat in the Travelift slings he sounded the bottom with a plastic mallet, finding no structural concerns and no blisters. Anstey, who had built boats in England and managed one of the largest yards in Ft. Lauderdale before turning to surveying, told Carl that the boat was an excellent choice for the serious sailing he had in mind. Motoring back to the slip, Carl could barely contain his excitement. He scrambled all over the boat, checking one feature and then the next. He had a hundred questions. Finally I gave him the helm and disappeared below. Glancing up at him through the companionway, I saw on his face an expression of pure joy. That's what a sailboat can do to a dreamer.

A few days later the papers were signed and the funds wired. In an e-mail to family and friends, Carl wrote, "Well, we closed the deal today. Carl is now the proud owner of a Lavranos 41. The boat is a 1994 model in very good condition and should be ready for 'any ocean' sailing in a week or two. What's next? Well, there are not many limits with this boat; it'll go anywhere. I am going to risk the wrath of the Gods and rename her *La Vie en Rose*." Louis Armstrong's version of the beautiful song made famous by French chanteuse Edith Piaf had long been one of Carl's favorites. Loosely translated, the title means "a life in shades of rose"; even more loosely, it hints at shades of perfection. It was that elusive perfection that Carl hoped his boat might reveal to him.

He was giddy. At 51 years old he had at last transformed his long-incubated dream into fiberglass, Dacron, aluminum, and stainless steel. Islandia was within reach, just over the horizon.

For once, Carl's life was turning up roses.

AN AGING SOLDIER

"Four elements and five
    Senses, and man a spirit in love
    Tangling through this spun slime
    To his nimbus bell cool kingdom come . . ."

                    Dylan Thomas, "Poem on His Birthday"

CARL'S optimistic one-week "get the boat ready" time frame stretched on for nearly two months. I tried to convince him that he needed to spend time sailing his boat, not working on it. Time on the water is what a new sailor needs most, time to discover the foibles of the boat, to find out what it needs and, more important, what it doesn't. But new sailors rarely accept this advice. They can't resist making daily pilgrimages to marine stores, replacing perfectly good equipment with the latest gizmos, flashing their credit cards like Pentagon purchasing agents. Nothing is too good or too costly for their newly acquired boats. Sterling Hayden, who was a better sailor than actor, had a bemused and, to my way of thinking, accurate view of the gold-plated yachting syndrome. In his classic seafaring book *Wanderer*, he wrote:

> *Yachtsmen are consumed with the notion that their boats must be one hundred percent sound. They are oblivious to the fact that the majority of the world's working vessels are plagued with rot. Yet these are the*

ships that do the work, year after year, no holds barred when it comes to weather.

By this time, the spring of 1998, I'd moved off my ketch and into a rented house a few blocks away, making an attempt at being a land person. My wife had started a business, and I was often on kid patrol. I was devoting most of my time to writing magazine articles, with only occasional deliveries and charters to maintain my sanity, and it was a struggle. Carl picked up on my simmering frustrations right away. He seemed flattered that I lived vicariously through him as he prepared his boat for world cruising. He would often make his way to the house after a sweltering day in the yard to grab a shower and a cold beer and soak up the air-conditioning. Despite his endless list of boat projects he usually maintained his good cheer, and would relate the day's travails with wry humor.

The afternoon he had *La Vie en Rose* painted on the stern quarters was a good one. A new name for his boat meant a new life for him. According to an old superstition it is bad luck to change a boat's name, but we celebrated with a barbecue in the backyard anyway.

Minding the steaks before a few other guests arrived, we chatted. Carl was in an expansive mood. Buying the boat had liberated him even as his headlong plunge into the cruising life, so long postponed, had surprised and terrified him. He could talk of little else, but I was weary of boat talk and steered the conversation toward more personal matters.

"So what's the real situation with this Shelley you keep talking about?"

Carl was coy about the women in his life. He was a natural-born flirt and let on that he'd rarely been lonely during the years between wives, yet I'd never seen him with a woman.

"She's your first wife's sister, but she sounds like she's more than that. You're always talking about her."

"Shel is just a friend, a really good friend," he replied, stretching the "really" just long enough to leave me wondering what it meant. "We used to joke that I should have married her instead—we really get along great, we always did. She's more like a sister than a sister-in-law. We were teenagers when we all met—well, at least the girls were. She's family to me. The best thing I ever did was not sever my relationships with my ex's family."

"What about your first wife?" I knew this was still a difficult subject, even many years after they'd divorced.

"What can I say about Sallie? She's beautiful, the most honest person I've ever known, brilliant. Now she even has money. She had no reason to stay with me."

It was a typical self-deprecating Carl response, designed to skirt the issue, to leave me guessing without wiggle room for further interrogation. Carl had worked hard to maintain a good relationship with Sallie, who had recently remarried, and I never heard him utter a disparaging remark about her. Yet it didn't take a shrink to see that the failure of their relationship haunted him. Sallie, not his second wife, Beatrice, was the woman of his dreams, the love of his life, and he had lost her. Carl desperately wanted to be philosophical about the past, to see his life as a canvas, its successes and failures given grace and meaning by splashes of wisdom and humor. He wanted to frame his life as a series of experiences that had led him, as if by plan, to the point where he was now—ready, at age 51, to judge and be judged by the standards of the sea. Yet broken glass littered his trail, and shards of it were embedded in his heart.

Carl had met Sallie when he was at Fort Belvoir, Virginia, attending the prep school there that served as a staging point for young adults headed to the United States Military Academy— West Point. That he was even a candidate for West Point was a small miracle; he had come in through the back door. After high school in Bradenton he had enlisted in the army, more to get away from home than for anything else. His parents had divorced when he was 3, and three years later his mother had married a man with whom Carl never got along. College seemed out of the question, extravagant, a place for rich kids— and there wasn't a lot of extra money floating around the Wake household. The army offered a ticket out of town, even if that road was likely to lead through Southeast Asia.

In those days, the mid-1960s, the army was actively recruit- ing and allowed a certain number of enlisted men to apply for entry into the academy. After serving in Korea, Carl was per- suaded by his superiors to apply to West Point, and to his com- plete surprise he was accepted, provided he complete a year at the Belvoir prep school first. He was not from an elite high school. He had not been a brilliant student. He was not a cham- pion athlete. He was a quiet, capable, dependable guy who had already proven himself in two years of military service. He was an idealist, and he believed in good and evil, right and wrong, and in doing his duty. In those respects, at least, he was just what the academy was looking for.

Sallie's father was an air force officer stationed at nearby Andrews Air Force Base, and Carl first spotted Sallie Hester at an on-base dance arranged for officers' daughters to make sure they met the right young men. They danced, sparks flew, and a long courtship began. They dated all through Carl's West Point years, even when Sallie went away to college. "Those were exciting years," Sallie recalls. "When Carl gave me his junior class ring, it was clear that we were going to get married."

But Carl's West Point years were not overly satisfying for him. Matriculating at 21, he was older and more experienced than most of his classmates and also an independent thinker, a trait that isn't encouraged at the academy. Having been raised like an only child—his sister being ten years older—Carl was also a loner, another characteristic frowned upon by professional soldiers. Depending on the man next to you in combat is a matter of life and death. A soldier prone to defining his duty before doing it is too much of a wild card in the army.

He had few close friends at West Point and was never part of a popular group or one of the guys—a pattern that would continue throughout his military career. His West Point roommate, Dave Kotzebue, remembers him as a bit of a rogue, a shameless womanizer, and a dear friend. "A lot of guys didn't like him because he hit on their girlfriends," Kotzebue said with a laugh. "I liked him because we respected each other's girl, but it was more than that. Once you got to know Carl, you found out he had a heart of gold. He would do anything for you. But he could push the envelope, and he could frustrate some of his superiors. He was a small town kid from Bradenton with big dreams and something to prove, and he wanted to do things his way."

Carl was an average student. "He did enough to get by," says Kotzebue, "but he always had strange ideas about things. He loved to talk philosophy. He could have been a brilliant student if he'd pushed himself." Carl was savvy enough to realize that the academy represented a golden opportunity, especially with the Vietnam War escalating. He was determined to put in his four years and get a commission. Kotzebue was surprised that Carl chose to make the military a career, but noted, "Carl always worked the angles. The military is not a bad life, and Carl did manage to get a cushy retirement from the army."

Carl once told me, only half in jest, that the best thing to come out of his West Point years was that he learned to sail—first on the Hudson River in a Sunfish, that ubiquitous small boat, then later, during a two-week exchange at the Naval Academy in his senior year, on the Chesapeake Bay. His midshipman roommate at Annapolis was a member of the Naval Academy sailing team, and Carl spent every afternoon and both weekends crisscrossing the bay on a 44-foot sloop. He fell in love with sailing. "I never forgot those wonderful days on the bay, but unfortunately I spent the next 20 years in the army," he told me in a letter, accounting for his limited sailing experience.

Shortly after being commissioned, Carl was posted to Germany and assigned to the 3rd Infantry, the "Rock of the Marne" division famed for a heroic stand during the bloodbath of World War I. There he oversaw the maintenance and deployment of heavy equipment, particularly generators. The military of the 1970s was a bastion of disillusionment, and the excitement of being overseas soon wore off. After four years of relentless and rigorous training at the Military Academy, day-to-day life in the army was mind-numbing. Carl was disgusted with the band of drugged-up dropouts under his command. He felt more like a highly trained babysitter than a freshly minted second lieutenant. Having joined the army in search of personal fulfillment and glory, he found himself adrift in a bureaucracy that was floundering in the wake of Vietnam failures and searching for an identity.

Carl and Sallie were married when she finished her degree at George Washington University. "We really had a lot of respect and love, but we were just so different," Sallie said. Carl's deliberate, consider-every-option mode of doing things drove his new bride crazy. Sallie was, in many ways, his opposite. She was intuitive, quick to grasp almost anything, and had a can-do attitude. According to her sister Shelley, Sallie had been mischievous and something of a lovable troublemaker as a kid. Once they were married, Carl adopted Sallie's family, including her little sister Shelley, and the Hesters adopted him in turn. "He was treated more like a son than a son-in-law," Shelley told me, echoing a phrase I'd heard from Carl years before. "Mom and Dad loved Carl," Sallie said. "He was the son they never had."

Carl was a frustrated soldier, looking for perfection and honor in a world of compromise and backbiting. Like all military couples, Carl and Sallie were transferred often. After three years in Mannheim, Germany, they returned to the D.C. area, which Sallie loved, and later moved to Fort Bragg, North Carolina, which she didn't. At Fort Bragg, Sallie began her career with the Department of Defense. As her flair and efficiency made her increasingly successful, she became less interested in sacrificing her career to follow Carl around the world. When Carl was sent back to Korea, she was transferred to Washington, D.C. "That's when our relationship started to slide. My career was going well, and I didn't really want to move to Korea." Carl and Sallie were living separate lives.

Although they rarely lived under the same roof after that, Carl thought for a while that starting a family might save their marriage. It was an odd notion, because he had conflicted emotions about children. "When he came back from Korea he wanted to have children," Sallie remembers, "but then in the same sentence he worried terribly about having a handicapped child. By that point I felt like our relationship was in serious trouble, and having a child would not make it better."

In the meantime, Shelley had married and had recently had a child. In a congratulatory letter, Carl told Shelley that he "personally did not want to bring children into the world. Kids deserved better than what the world was offering." Shelley was never sure whether that was Carl's genuine belief or merely a rationalization for a childless marriage. Years later he would become a doting uncle, and he was likewise very fond of my two children, showering them with presents. As with many issues in his life, Carl seems never to have resolved these tangled feelings.

But children represent the ultimate commitment, and despite a career in the army, Carl was not well suited for commitment. When he returned from Korea he was stationed at Fort Stewart, near Savannah, Georgia, and he and Sallie decided that it was time to part ways.

Fourteen years after graduating from West Point, Carl had attained the rank of lieutenant colonel. His military career was plodding along—as he put it, "nothing spectacular but not too bad either." He was never going to make general, but he had the grudging respect of his superiors. According to Dave Kotzebue, Carl was never well liked in the army, but his competence made up for what he lacked in zeal. He believed that he was smarter than his commanding officers and had difficulty hiding his scorn. The younger Carl wore condescension like a medal.

In the spring of 1985 he was 39 years old and had logged almost twenty years, including his early service and time at West Point. He had renovated a few houses on the side and had some money. He was comfortable but not happy, his ambitions smoldering behind the façade of a dutiful soldier. He was just doing his time.

A moderate drinker and heavy smoker, Carl was nevertheless lean and fit, yet he found himself struggling to keep up on the morning 5-mile runs on base that spring. One day he not only couldn't keep up, he couldn't keep going. He dropped out of the run. At first it didn't seem like an emergency, but he was having a hard time catching his breath. He went home, where, stripping off his clothes for a shower, he suddenly had pains in his chest—terrible pains—and then collapsed. Later he wasn't sure how long he had lain on the floor, and when he came to it took him a moment to realize that he wasn't dead. The pains had subsided. He called 911 and was rushed to the hospital. His blood pressure was through the roof, and an EKG confirmed that Carl had suffered a serious heart attack. The doctor told him he was lucky to be alive.

After his condition stabilized he was flown to Fort Sam Houston, near San Antonio, Texas. There he underwent triple bypass surgery at Brooke Army Medical Center, a facility that specializes in amputations and prostheses and twenty years later would be dealing with injured Iraq War veterans. Even at one of the military's premier medical centers, open-heart surgery was considered a high-risk operation in 1985, but with the help of his relative youth and general good health, Carl came through the operation well. Along with the need to quit smoking, his doctors prescribed another change—a change in attitude. There was no doubt that stress had contributed to the attack. His marriage had failed, his career was stalled, and his youthful ideals were shattered. It was time for him to change his life.

His roommate at Brooke was an older man who had also undergone open-heart surgery, but Carl was more interested in the lovely young woman standing at the older man's bedside.

"We made eye contact and the magic went from there," Sue Reynolds told me. "He and my daddy shared a room. He was in Texas for about a month, and by the time he went home to Georgia, we both knew that we had something special." When Carl was well enough to return home, the army did the honorable thing, crediting him with twenty years of active service and putting him out to pasture with 80 percent disability pay.

As Carl rehabilitated, he and Sue began writing, and soon their correspondence grew torrid. Once he felt up to it Carl visited her in California, and a passionate love affair blossomed. Still, geography and Carl's need to heal his emotional wounds kept them from fully committing to each other. Carl was untethered for the first time in his adult life. The army was all he'd known, and, until Sue, Sallie was the only woman he'd loved. He didn't know what to do with his time. After his heart attack, his very notion of time had changed. He didn't know how much longer he might live.

This way of thinking was not in Carl's nature, and it didn't last, but it did prevent him from establishing a committed relationship with Sue. His heart was literally and figuratively vulnerable. He kept his guard up, albeit in a charming way. He sent Sue heartfelt letters, but there was always an out, a reason why they couldn't be together full-time. Sue carried on with her life, but they remained close and had occasional rendezvous for years.

Yet when Carl finally decided to chance marriage again, he picked Bea, for reasons he probably did not fully understand. Bea would not turn out to be a soul mate, but perhaps at the time their personality differences were what attracted him most. To a man seeking to change his life, Bea represented a distinct break with the past.

Nevertheless, Carl and Sue continued to stay in touch. They were each other's confidants, and what had begun as a love affair transformed itself into an enduring friendship. Sue would later say that they were planning to sail together once Carl made it over to her side of the country, to see if it was time to resume their long-simmering romance. Maybe Carl was leading her on, or maybe not. Carl needed Sue. She was his connection to past and present worlds. She loved him in the way Carl needed to be loved, without judging or demanding commitment. And she accepted the solitude at the core of his existence.

NEVER ON FRIDAY

"At rest on a stair landing,
   They feel it
   Moving beneath them now like the deck of a ship,
   Though the swell is gentle."

Donald Justice, "Men at Forty"

By the time Carl relaunched *La Vie en Rose* in April 1998, I had little time to lend a hand. The original plan had been for me to sail with him from Ft. Lauderdale to Bradenton, a 250-mile shakedown cruise via the Florida Keys, but I had article deadlines, a boat to deliver, and kids to look after. We compromised: I'd sail as far as Marathon in the Keys, and he'd press on from there alone. A blustery northeast wind greeted us as we cleared the breakwalls at Port Everglades and turned right. With a cool breeze curving the sails, we zipped south, eating away the 100 miles to Marathon, an overnight sail.

When Carl took the helm I was surprised to see how he oversteered, spinning the wheel furiously after each lumpy wave passed under the keel. I assumed he just needed to get used to the boat, and reminded myself that he hadn't sailed since the sea trial. The sun slipped behind the glittering sky-scrapers of Miami's Brickle Avenue, and while a canopy of stars reached down to the sea, placing us at the center of the universe, Carl found his stride at the helm. He wasn't ready to drive an America's Cup boat, but he was doing much better—which was a good thing, because the autopilot wasn't working.

This was a serious problem, as self-steering gear is vital for singlehanded sailing. It is impossible to hand steer a boat day and night. The autopilot would need to be repaired in Marathon. Hoisting a mug of coffee, I welcomed Carl to the world of cruising—the fine art of repairing boat equipment in exotic locations.

Reduced to hand steering, our overnight watch system collapsed. Instead we traded the helm every hour and talked through the night. I brewed another pot of coffee and slapped together a couple of sandwiches.

Tucked beneath the spray dodger, I confessed that my marriage was troubled and that I was finding it difficult to maintain a dual existence, with one foot ashore and one aboard. I rambled on about how I wanted to sail off with my kids, to raise them on a diet of self-reliance, salt water, and world culture. I felt like a failure because this dream was slipping through my fingers. My wife was weary of my dreams and, worse, downright sick of my realities. If our marriage collapsed, or more likely when it collapsed, my plans of sailing the world with my kids would be reduced to part-time cruising at best.

Carl was a patient man—it was one of his finest attributes. He knew full well where my marriage was heading—he was, after all, a specialist in broken relationships—but he was too much of a gentleman to press the issue. He didn't need to prove how smart he was by forecasting the misery that awaited me, maybe not that year or the next, but soon enough. Instead he turned the conversation inward, to the issue we always wound our way back to, the slippery nature of personal freedom. No wonder our marriages never lasted—we both kept a foot in the door and wondered where the draft was coming from.

He took a contemplative drag on his cigarette—he had cut down on his smoking in the years after his heart attack but was never able to kick the habit completely. Then he pitched it overboard and began to speak in a soft voice.

"Men kill and readily die for freedom, but does anyone truly understand what they're fighting for? I felt that it was my duty to fight for freedom—that's what we were trained to do in the army—but I came to see that I was anything but free. What was I fighting for then?" Carl's military metaphors caught me off guard. He rarely spoke of his army past. "This boat represents ultimate freedom for me, but freedom from what? From past failures, from comparisons to my West Point classmates, from the scorn of my ex-wives? I don't know. I'm still trying to figure that one out."

He talked of duty and how difficult it was to find the right path in life, especially when you had to figure it out for yourself. *Duty* struck me as a quaint, overly simplistic concept, which Carl claimed clearly identified me as a child of the '60s and '70s. "Duty meant something to me when I was young," he said. But duty and freedom were, in his words, "oil and water."

"At least you know where you belong," he said. "You belong out here. This is where you're at your best. You know it, but you just won't admit it because the consequences are too painful. Tell me it doesn't come down to freedom versus duty? It always does." He drew out the "always," emphasizing both syllables in his pronounced Southern drawl.

"As for me," he continued, "I don't belong anywhere. Sometimes I think I am a misfit in this world. I have made the shift from a type A to type B personality, but sometimes that just leaves me wondering if I am really a type C—none of the above." I couldn't imagine Carl ever having been a true type A, aggressively competitive, but I knew he was speaking of his escape from the career military treadmill. He paused, framing the words. "I am truly hoping that sailing and cruising will lead me not away from the world but somehow back into it, to help me find where I belong. This is where I want to be. I am just hoping that I can make it out here."

I had little doubt Carl would make it. Offshore sailing requires an uneasy mixture of moxie and humility; Carl had the latter, and I was sure he had the former, too. But what of my duty? Carl was right: out here was where I belonged. Was my duty to my children destined to keep me from the one place I was truly comfortable? The question tormented me through the night.

We made landfall the next morning, hastily removed the autopilot drive unit, and dropped it off at the shop. Then I hurried home. It took just a day for the autopilot to be repaired, and Carl shoved off the following morning. Almost as soon as he left Marathon the autopilot failed again, but he didn't turn back, hand steering hours on end instead. The day was bright and the night was clear. He was alone on the ocean, enchanted. Twelve hours of steering was an inconvenience, not a catastrophe. Then he snagged a lobster pot float line on his engine propeller.

After struggling and failing to free the tangled mess with a boathook, he reluctantly concluded that he had no option but to go overboard and cut the line by hand. It's unnerving to leave your boat under any circumstance, but especially so when you're alone and on your first passage. He was just 10 miles offshore, but he might as well have been in the middle of the Gulf of Mexico.

He finally mustered the nerve to make the plunge after listening to the harried calls of weekend boaters on the VHF radio. One after another they hailed Sea Tow and TowBoatU.S., the AAA outfits of the Intracoastal Waterway, for assistance with minor boating problems. If he was going to be a successful world cruiser, he couldn't let a snagged lobster pot stop him. He tied a safety line around his waist, slipped over the side, cut the pot line, and scrambled back aboard. He said later that being in the water felt like being on a space walk. He was exhausted and exhilarated by the time he reached Regatta Pointe Marina on the Manatee River, where he promptly ran aground off the marina entrance. "A fitting way to end my first voyage," he wrote in his web log.

When Carl had chosen Bradenton as his initial destination— even before selling his house and buying *La Vie en Rose*—the main reason had been to be close to his mother. Now his mother was dead, but he followed the plan anyway. His first task upon arrival in Bradenton was to move Bijou aboard. He was devoted to the sandy-haired retriever to a degree that non-dog people found difficult to comprehend.

Shortly after, Al Davis turned up for a week of sailing. Carl had met Al the year before during my boat-buying workshop. A retired high school principal, Al was contemplating a cruising sabbatical but wasn't yet ready to commit to the demands of boat ownership. In the meantime he was happy to join Carl and help him prepare *La Vie* for her upcoming voyage.

Al told me after their short trip up into Tampa Bay that he was a bit surprised at Carl's lack of expertise handling the boat, but that Carl's enthusiasm for cruising was infectious. They struck a deal. Al would join Carl from time to time to satiate his sailing desire and to provide an occasional but welcome hand. Carl was certainly not philosophically or emotionally committed to solo sailing—he was just resigned to the necessity and determined to keep that sad fact from squashing his dreams. His former sister-in-law Shelley believes that Carl's sailing dreams were so precious, so long incubated, that he preferred not to be tortured by a mate's less-than-complete commitment. He was open to having friends, family, and any willing romantic interests join him as occasional crew, but he didn't care to risk the success of his dreams on anyone else's unpredictable psyche—his own was unpredictable enough. He'd waited too long already, and a part of him liked the sympathy and awe that he evoked when he told people he was sailing alone.

After Al flew home to Illinois, Carl settled into life at Regatta Pointe, becoming a regular at the Riverside Café, the harborside bar and restaurant on the marina grounds. Other friends joined him for short coastal hops, including Tom Criste. The two men daysailed down the coast, and although Tom was seriously ill with cancer, he managed to spend four days aboard. They made vague plans to rendezvous in the Caribbean islands once Carl shoved off on his big voyage, a reunion cruise to celebrate those wonderful, carefree days they'd spent together in the Virgin Islands a decade before. They both knew those plans would go unfulfilled, but just making them was important to both.

Spring stretched into summer, and by the time Carl was ready to head south, hurricane season was in full swing. He decided to stay put, and drove rather than sailed down to Ft. Lauderdale in August for my fortieth birthday party. This event was a complete surprise to me, with friends from all over the world turning up to help me celebrate over-the-hilldom. I was happy to have Carl there with my best chums. We caroused late into the night, and Carl cut loose. The beer and Baileys flowed, and he thoroughly enjoyed himself. He was the life of the party. It was a side of Carl I had not seen before.

Carl finally left Regatta Pointe on his first extended cruise in late October 1998, sailing down the coast and then overnight to the Dry Tortugas. "Boy, I love sailing at night!" he wrote. "Next time you're out at night, raise your hand and guess how many stars you can cover . . . then add another thousand when you're over the horizon, away from the nearest lights." A handful of sandspits, some barely above water, the Dry Tortugas are home to Fort Jefferson, a national monument that consumes nearly all of Garden Key. This massive structure proves that pork-barrel spending was alive and well in Congress in the mid-1800s. It made no sense to build the largest, most expensive fort in the country on a sandspit that could easily be avoided by enemy ships. It served as part of the Union blockade during the Civil War, but the boys in blue never managed to fire a shot at the rebels. It became an expensive prison and later saw use as a staging point during the Spanish-American War in 1898.

Perched 70 miles west of Key West, the well-protected reef-fringed harbor that lies in the shadow of the great brick fort makes a terrific landfall, but things went wrong for Carl from the start. He tried to enter the silted-in north channel and went aground. Then, after he made his way into the anchorage, the wind whipped up and he spent two long days and nights dragging and resetting his anchor and fretting over it. By the time the wind dropped he was exhausted.

His next port of call was Key West, where he arrived during Fantasy Fest, a week of no-holds-barred revelry and debauchery. Fantasy gave way to reality a week later, however, when the remnants of Hurricane Mitch came calling. Mitch, a ferocious Category 5 storm, had demolished Honduras with wind and rains that resulted in floods and mudslides and left 18,000 people dead or missing. Mitch then lost steam and lurched into the Yucatán Straits. It was at tropical storm strength when it angled toward the Florida Keys, but it was still packing a wallop.

Carl rode out the storm in the anchorage near Garrison Bight, just off downtown Key West. He had two anchors set as Mitch rocked Key West with 45- to 50-knot winds. All went well until one anchor rode wrapped around a channel mark, but luckily the line held. The most harrowing moment came the next day when Carl took Bijou ashore to do his business. The winds were still howling, and the seas were white with foam. On the ride back, Bijou—all 85 pounds of him—managed to get between Carl and the outboard motor, and wave after wave crashed over them as Carl conned the small inflatable boat back to *La Vie en Rose*. Bijou was reluctant to leave the pitching dinghy when they drew alongside, and Carl was forced to heave the dog on deck. After he secured the dinghy and climbed exhaustedly aboard, Bijou topped off the adventure with a shaking frenzy that showered Carl with salt water again. But Bijou was beyond reproach. Carl loved him like the son he'd never had.

After the storm, Carl gathered himself, put *La Vie* in order, and set sail for Ft. Lauderdale. He made brief stops in Marathon and Long Key, primarily for Bijou's sake—as the dog refused to relieve himself on board—before tying up at the city docks. I stopped by for a visit after picking up my girls from school. I was proud of him as he told me of his ordeal in the Dry Tortugas and how he had ridden out Hurricane Mitch. He had come a long way as a sailor.

I had a few stories of my own. I too had taken a beating from Mitch. I'd been delivering a 46-foot sloop "down island" when Mitch re-formed after blasting Key West. It was a full-fledged hurricane again when it overran us east of the Bahamas. The seas were colossal, and the winds peaked at 80 knots as the eye passed just to the north. We rode out the storm under deeply reefed sails, terrified. "At one point I was at the helm for 18 hours," I told him.

"You always have to outdo me, don't you?" Carl replied, with a laugh tinged by storm envy. Instantly I felt stupid. I should have kept my mouth shut.

"So you were in the heart of it, the heart of the storm?" Carl queried.

"Well, I don't know about that, but it was pretty bad out there."

"One day I want to experience the heart of a storm, but not until I have a few more miles under my belt."

"So how long are you in town for?" I asked, anxious to change the subject.

"I have three weeks. Then I'm going to head back to Bradenton to leave the boat. I'll spend the holidays in Atlanta. My sister is real sick and I want to spend some time with her—don't know how much longer she'll be around. I want to make sure I see everybody I should see before I take off for parts unknown."

"Well, you know you're always welcome at the house. The girls would love to play with Bijou in the backyard. We can fire up the barbecue."

"I'll be by, but first I think I'll visit my favorite beach bar and hopefully my favorite waitress. You know the Quarterdeck's just a few blocks away. But I don't want you to think that's why I picked this marina."

Carl alluded to a number of favorite beach bars and restaurants, with their waitresses and female bartenders, both in his web log and in the long letters he sent me and a few other close friends. Besides the waitress at the Quarterdeck, there was the bartender at the Riverside Café in Regatta Pointe, a waitress at Miller's Marina on Boca Grande, and the bartender at Pepe's in Key West. I was never sure if these women were mere acquaintances—a good bartender can make any sailor feel like he's just one more drink away from a late-night house call—or something more. Perhaps one or two received personal tours of *La Vie en Rose*'s cabin, but Carl seemed lonely.

He admitted—and his West Point roommate, Dave Kotzebue, confirmed—that he had been a flirt and a womanizer once, but at age 52, adrift between past failures and a halting dream, he was looking more for companionship than a romp in the sack. He was also desperately trying to act his age. His girl-in-every-port intimations might have been, in part, attempts to reassure friends, and perhaps himself too, that a solo sailor need not be a recluse.

Carl at his most expansive could make any man or woman feel like his best friend, yet when he retreated to his natural repose, it was one of solitude. He had always been a loner, but being alone is something else again. Even—or especially—as he plotted a distant orbit, he needed a tether to the world he would be leaving behind. Friends, when kept at arm's length, could provide that connection without threatening his private self.

He was corresponding regularly with Sue Reynolds in California. Both were at loose ends, and they kept their vague plan in place to rendezvous once Carl transited the Panama Canal. But Carl's exact itinerary—even his rough itinerary—changed with the tides. He seemed determined not to be pinned down by expectations. A pursuit of freedom was, after all, the biggest attraction of voyaging. And there was always the specter of Sallie Hester, his first wife, and her family—particularly Shelley, her sister. One or the other is mentioned in a disproportionate number of his e-mails and letters. Carl could never quite disengage from the Hesters; it was with them that he felt most comfortable.

After a three-week stay in Ft. Lauderdale, Carl made his way back to Key West. "The more time I spend in this town, the more I like it," he wrote. Bijou liked it too. He was able to roam in and out of the open-air shops and laid-back bars without reprimand. Carl wrote that he would consider making Key West his home base after his world cruise. After a short stay he carried on to Bradenton and left the boat in the marina, driving his van to Atlanta. After the holidays it would be time to get serious; he had to make final preparations before he shoved off for good. He fully expected many years to pass before he sailed back up the Manatee River.

Carl was in a funk when he returned from Atlanta. He knew his sister Pat was dying, *La Vie's* rudder needed what he thought was a serious repair, and he was lonelier than ever. He had left Bijou with his niece in Atlanta, partly because he'd read that dogs were not welcome in Panama and partly because, now that he had settled on his route for the first year out, he felt it wouldn't be fair to confine Bijou to the boat. He had decided to sail south to Mexico, then continue down the Caribbean coast of Central America to Panama. Once through the canal, he planned to make two long tacks through the Pacific. The first would take him out toward the Hawaiian Islands, and the second would carry him back to the California coast. It was an ambitious plan—especially the last part, which amounted to a 5,000-mile nonstop passage. He'd never before sailed more than 150 miles at one time.

The faulty rudder, which was at the core of the autopilot problems, proved to be a minor repair, only requiring new bearings and an adjustment where the rudder stock entered the hull. Carl hauled the boat at a local yard and was back in the water within a week. His nephew Noel, a skilled marine mechanic, was Carl's angel while the boat was in Bradenton. Noel oversaw the rudder repair and helped with other items on Carl's never-shrinking project list.

Sadly, Carl's sister Pat—Noel's mother—passed away in early February. Pat had been one of his final links to land. It was time to begin his voyage, but still he stalled. "Boy, it's hard to cut loose from land," he wrote on March 1, 1999. "A trillion tiny threads holding you back. Spent this week cutting those threads like a combine through a wheatfield." In truth, it was more as if he was wielding a pair of scissors. He was having a difficult time wrapping up his affairs, and he tarried over insignificant issues. Carl was a master procrastinator and not always one to finish a job. When he'd sailed into Ft. Lauderdale, only the starboard side teak had been refinished. He'd run out of enthusiasm by the time he reached the port side.

Finally, when Al Davis arrived in Bradenton on March 8, Carl had no choice but to push off from the dock. The great adventure had begun—sort of. Their first waypoint was just a few miles away from the marina, the dock at Moore's Stone Crab restaurant. Two days later they ambled down the coast to Gasparilla Island. Al left the boat there, and Carl was on his own. He made his next stop Key West.

In Key West Carl purchased courtesy flags for visiting Cuba, Mexico, Belize, Honduras, Costa Rica, Colombia, and Panama.

He wasn't certain he'd stop in all those countries, but he wanted to be prepared. He went to the Naval Hospital in Key West and received yellow fever, hepatitis A, and typhoid shots. He made his way to Pepe's several times and visited with other cruisers. On March 27 he finally hauled his anchor and headed west, stopping briefly in the Dry Tortugas—another familiar landfall—before pushing on for Isla Mujeres (the "isle of women") just off the Yucatán coast near Cancún. This would be his first foreign landfall.

By the second night of the passage he was battling fierce headwinds and a contrary current. He stayed up all night, and the weather improved with sunrise. Four long days out from the Dry Tortugas, *La Vie en Rose* negotiated the pass through the reef and dropped anchor in the lagoon at Isla Mujeres. Carl was exhausted but excited; he felt that he was finally living his dream. "In three weeks we are already 500 miles from our home port (Bradenton), half the distance we did all last year!" Reading his message, I thought of what my mother, a circumnavigator, had told me: Passagemaking is like pregnancy—when it's over, all you remember is the satisfaction of making landfall, not the pain of long night watches and wayward autopilots.

"Can't believe I dropped anchor 50 feet from probably the only female singlehander in the Caribbean," Carl wrote in his log, and he may have been right. This solo sailor was a 33-year-old British woman named Debbie. She was tall and blonde and sailing with her dog, and she and Carl made an immediate connection. Carl was impressed that she was able to handle a 45-foot boat by herself. Debbie had been in Isla Mujeres for several weeks and showed Carl around town. She also helped him sew his torn headsail. Carl never revealed whether this friendship blossomed into something more, but he made an abrupt course change when Debbie headed south from Isla Mujeres. Instead of carrying south toward Panama as planned, he decided that his autopilot was too unreliable and chose instead to sail back to Key West. It was a curious decision, one he never fully explained. He may have reasoned that it was too late in the year to head for the Pacific—that he wouldn't be able to sail toward Hawaii before the onset of hurricane season—but the same day Debbie cleared for Belize, he sailed the other way. Three days later he was anchored off Garrison Bight, back in Key West once again.

Carl spent two weeks there, visiting friends, feeling at home. "This is really a crossroads for me," he wrote. In another about-face, he decided to sail up the East Coast for the summer. It was early May, the perfect time to head north. He sailed first to Ft. Lauderdale, then on to Cape Canaveral and finally to St. Augustine, visiting sailing friends in each harbor along the way. I never imagined that our dinner at the Quarterdeck would be the last time I'd see him.

Carl was settling into the cruising lifestyle and becoming increasingly comfortable on *La Vie en Rose*. He often wrote that he "loved this boat," and he never missed an opportunity to thank me for helping him find it and for encouraging him to buy it.

On the afternoon of May 26 he cleared St. Augustine Inlet bound for the mouth of the Chesapeake Bay, a 500-mile non-stop passage via Cape Hatteras. This was the open ocean sailing Carl had been imagining for years. The winds were light but steady, the Gulf Stream current, setting north, was a magic carpet adding a couple of extra knots to *La Vie*'s 5-knot speed. Dolphins were frequent visitors, and Carl discovered that they preferred Pink Floyd to Jimmy Buffett as he blasted the stereo for their amusement. He was able to sleep in short intervals during the evening and longer stretches in daylight. He always slept in the cockpit. The autopilot kept a steady grip on the helm. He grew more proficient at tuning in the weather forecasts on the single-sideband radio, and the radar provided occasional glimpses beyond the dark horizon. The weather was ideal. The full moon shed so much light that he drifted around dreaded Cape Hatteras—the infamous "grave-yard of the Atlantic"—while sprawled out in the cockpit reading at midnight.

"This passage is like a good book. You don't want it to end," Carl wrote. He had found his stride as a solo sailor. "This is one of the best times I've had on the water. I really, REALLY like open-water sailing." The winds came up from the south as he entered the Chesapeake, giving him a cracking reach into the bay. He finally dropped anchor in Fishing Bay, near Deltaville in southern Virginia. That night Carl wrote that he was "feeling supremely content." Sitting at the nav station, punching away on his laptop, he continued:

I really know how blessed I am tonight, and I give thanks for each of these wonderful days. I think of all the bad things that have happened these past few years; that's the luck of it, or fate, or Karma, or whatever. It is all about fate versus free will. It seems to me that what-ever forces run this place, they make it a combination maze and obstacle course. If we insist on free will and self-determination we can only find it by really focusing ourselves. As we run our course we cannot avoid the obstacles and bombshells that come our way—that's fate again, and it always has a surprise in store. But if we

hope to find that sense of self, of self-determination, we
must do it in the gaps when Fate is busy somewhere else.
It is far too easy to get confused and take off on the wrong
path. There are an infinite number of ways to face tomor-
row; to make it the path WE desire, that is the challenge.

He was rambling, trying in his humble way to say that he
was proud of himself. After a relaxing stay in Fishing Bay, Carl
sailed up the Chesapeake Bay to Annapolis, from where he flew
to Atlanta, returning with Bijou. Now he had all the pieces in
place for happiness—well, almost. He wrote to me that most
cruisers he met were couples, and despite Bijou's return, he was
still feeling lonely. Still, a part of him enjoyed a bit of martyr-
dom, which he kept neatly wrapped in a layer of stoicism. He
also coped with loneliness by not tarrying in port. He was more
than making up for his lazy first year aboard. While other cruisers lingered in anchorages for weeks, Carl kept moving. He
made his way through the Chesapeake and Delaware Canal and
back into the open waters of the Atlantic.

Carl spent three days anchored off Sandy Hook, a sliver of
sand reaching off the Jersey shore that locals say is giving the
finger to New York City to the north. When he finally sum-
moned the courage to tackle the hustle, bustle, and extreme
currents of New York Harbor, it turned out to be anticlimactic.
He slipped past Liberty Island, South Street Seaport, and the
Brooklyn Bridge early in the morning, then, timing the tide perfectly, sluiced through Hell Gate, where the East and Harlem
rivers meet and the currents can run at more than 7 knots. By
noon he was anchored off City Island at the foot of Long Island
Sound. He made a quick tour of the sound before heading for
Provincetown, on Cape Cod, and there he slowed down.

Carl had offered a few days aboard to Monique, his friend Tom Criste's widow. Carl and Tom had competed for Monique's attention years before, and although she had married Tom, Carl, in characteristic fashion, had remained close to both. Now he could offer Monique a respite from her grief while sharing memories of a man they both had loved. Perhaps he also entertained notions of a rekindled romance, or perhaps not. In any case, Carl also made another connection in Provincetown, a woman named Maria who ran a little breakfast spot on the wharf. After Monique's visit he continued north, visiting the Isles of Shoals off New Hampshire's bite-sized coastline.

On August 30, 1999, Carl turned south. His newest plan was to hop his way along the coast back to the Chesapeake Bay. From there, he'd wait until the tail end of hurricane season before heading offshore for the long passage to the Caribbean. A few days later he anchored off the breakwater in Provincetown again. Ensconced at his favorite dockside table at Maria's café, Carl received a call from his niece Rebecca. Pat's husband Guy, who had been more like a brother than a brother-in-law, had passed away. Carl returned to Atlanta for the funeral, his fifth in two years, then hurried back to the boat to be aboard as Hurricane Floyd flirted with a New England landfall.

Floyd spared *La Vie*, and by early October Carl had made his way back to Annapolis. He lingered in the Naval Shipyard there, making final preparations for his first "real," as he called it, blue-water passage. "This will be my first passage of more than 1,000 miles," he wrote. "It will be good to get this one under my belt." While in Annapolis he learned that my mother had recently passed away. Death seemed to be shadowing him. He sent me a letter:

Dear John,

Found out you lost your mother just a week or so before my brother-in-law died. So sorry. Boy, I liked your Mom. I remember the day you brought her to see La Vie. *I wasn't sure what to expect, but within a few minutes it was obvious she was one of those grand ladies that makes everyone feel comfortable. What a woman—she would be equally comfortable eating peel-and-eat shrimp in a Mexican beach bar or accepting a lift to the airport in the Kennedys' limo. What a blessing to be raised by a woman like that. All you can do is try to be the son she was so proud of.*

On October 29 he left Annapolis, bound for Fishing Bay. From there he'd wait for a clear weather window to head offshore. Just before he left he sent an e-mail to everybody on his list:

Hi All,

Will be in Fishing Bay tomorrow. From there it's just a few hours to the mouth of the Chesapeake Bay. Have been keeping an eye on the weather the last few days— expecting Tropical Storm Katrina to be off Charleston, SC, on Tuesday and past Cape Hatteras late Tuesday. There are a couple of other systems out there that could impact my trip . . . looks like a Wednesday or Thursday departure. Will certainly try to give you a "good-bye" message as I sail over the horizon, but I wanted to remind everyone that I will be out of touch a lot in the next few months. I should be in St. Thomas by mid-November and will spend a couple of weeks there. Once I leave there you probably won't hear from me directly

until April, when I'm due in California. I will find a way
to get some updates to Shelley so you can always check
the website for the last sighting!

This was the last direct correspondence most of Carl's
friends would ever receive from him. He waited in Fishing Bay
until the weather cleared. Then a cold front stalled, and he
delayed taking off on November 4. Instead he left the next day,
Friday, November 5, 1999.

For centuries superstitious sailors have avoided leaving port
on a Friday, calling it bad luck. The notion even made it into
insurers' actuarial tables: In sailing ship days, Lloyd's of London
would cancel its coverage of any vessel that it learned had set
sail on a Friday. I don't consider myself superstitious, but I too
have delayed departures until 1 minute after midnight to avoid
the wrath of Neptune. Why take a chance? But after a summer
and fall of tropical storms marauding across the Atlantic, and
with forecasters predicting particularly fierce winter storms
that year, Carl reasoned that a fair-weather window was more
important than a superstition.

ENGLISH BRAIDS

"The first night out was, as it always is, the loneliest of the passage. I have found when single-handed that the longer I am at sea the less I feel the loneliness and the more company I find in the sky, the wind, the waves, my boat and even in myself. But this night the sense of loneliness was accentuated by the weather, by periods of calm and slatting canvas punctuated with gale force squalls and icy rain. The dawn, thin as it was, was welcome."

Bill Howell, *White Cliffs to Coral Reefs*

FROM his dock space near the Lightship Restaurant, Simon Rigby had a perfect view of the Statue of Liberty across the park and the twin towers of the World Trade Center across the harbor. It was the spring of 1998, and Simon and his two German shepherds were living aboard his 41-foot ketch *Escape* at the Liberty Landing Marina in Jersey City. He was preparing the boat for serious ocean cruising, hell-bent on sailing home to Australia. When his younger brother Steve arrived unexpectedly, fresh from his latest travel adventure, the dogs went to Simon's ex-wife and Steve moved into the forward cabin. Steve soon found work as an instructor at Steve and Doris Colgate's Offshore Sailing School, the New York branch of which was located in the marina.

"It was great having Steve on the boat. We really had a nice gig going," Simon said later. "It wasn't like Ft. Lauderdale, where living aboard is no big deal. Living on a sailboat seemed to intrigue people in the Northeast, especially women. Liberty Landing was the perfect spot, too; we were just a short ferry ride from Manhattan, but we could escape the hubbub and retreat back to the boat. Life was good. We got a lot of mileage out of our accents, if you know what I mean. In those days, everyone wanted to see our knives, as if all Aussies were Crocodile Dundee. Steve and I were real close, brothers and best friends. I'm sure that sounds a bit contrived, but it was true. And Steve helped me a lot with the boat; he was more of a sailor than I'll ever be."

Christian Pschorr, head Offshore Sailing School instructor at the time, hired Steve despite his lack of professional experience. "He was very personable and turned out to be a great instructor too. He didn't have much of a sailing résumé but he had a passion about sailing that was obvious and infectious." Pschorr, who also lived in the marina at the time—aboard a tiny 29-foot sloop with his wife and two young sons—remembers Steve Rigby fondly. They were more than coworkers; they were good friends:

He was slim and fit, and despite a company policy that insisted he wear a uniform he always found a way to take off his shirt and reveal his six-pack abs. He looked a lot younger than he was. He was charming, and his ever-present smile framed crooked yellow teeth. He was definitely a ladies' man; women always wanted him to be their instructor. There was something about him, his accent, even his teeth—they were so far gone

they were cute. And of course his smile. He was impos-
sible not to like. Everyone liked Steve, even when he
made a mess of things.

Steven Rigby had been born in Stratford-on-Avon, Shakespeare's hometown, in 1957. Simon described his brother as restless and stubborn. Steve couldn't wait to leave the Bard's tourist trap behind and get out into the wide world. He had big dreams. He was the fourth of five children, and until age 15 he suffered the normal life of an English schoolboy. Then his life took a sharp and decidedly better turn. He was accepted as an apprentice at the prestigious stable of equestrian legend Fulke Walwyn, in Surrey.

"Steven always was a great lover of animals," his mother, Pat, explained. "At an early age he professed his desire to be a jockey, and he always followed his dreams. He kept writing and writing until Walwyn finally took him in."

"Steve could charm horses just like he could charm ladies," Simon said with a laugh. "He had a way with animals."

"I know it seems like a stretch to go from the stables to the sea," Pschorr says. "Yet Steve was like a thoroughbred on the water. He was erratic at the helm, but when he got it all together he was good."

Steve wanted to be a steeplechaser and a jump rider, not just a flat rider. Jumpers require great athleticism as well as an almost un-canny ability to communicate with their horse. All the leading jockeys in England had been jump racers once, and Steve intended to be a champion rider. He didn't lack self-confidence, and neither did Fulke Walwyn. Walwyn had been a champion jockey, winning England's premier event, the Grand National, in 1936. A tragic fall cut his riding career short, so he turned to training. When Steve arrived at his stables in the summer of 1972, Walwyn was widely regarded as one of the best jump trainers of all time.

Unfortunately, Steve started growing. Although he wasn't a big kid by ordinary standards, he was soon too tall to be a jockey. It was a keen disappointment—a dream shattered by something over which he had no control. "It was a blow to Steven, that jockey business," Pat told me, "but Steve always landed on his feet." His mother understood her son's ability to switch gears, to channel his passion in another direction once a dream flamed out. Steve's restless nature drove some people crazy, but it served him well.

By the time Steve left Walwyn's stable in 1974, Simon had emigrated to Australia and had convinced his parents to follow him there. Steve soon went as well. "Steve was always following me," Simon said years later, joking. Turning serious, he added, "I wish he was still here to follow me out into the Pacific." He looked around the cabin of *Escape*. He was docked in Ft. Lauderdale, en route to Panama and, eventually, Australia. "We should be sailing this boat home together. It would have been fitting."

The Rigbys settled in Queensland, where Steve followed Walwyn's lead and became a horse trainer. "He was definitely a top trainer," Simon told me, his pride obvious. He became a fixture at the leading tracks in Sydney and Melbourne, and his horses and riders were regulars in the winner's circle. But there was a dark side to the racing business. Christian Pschorr told me that when Steve had a few drinks in him and was feeling expansive, he would occasionally let slip that he had been involved in a few shady dealings in Australia and had to leave racing and the country. Whether he was forced from the business or was embellishing his past is hard to tell, but after fifteen years as a trainer he gave up horses and took to the road.

Steve was in his early thirties by then and eager to see the world beyond the barn. He traveled to Southeast Asia and Europe, but an extended trip to the Indian subcontinent influenced him most. Traveling from Sri Lanka through India to Nepal, Steve became intrigued with Buddhism. He was adrift, searching for meaning and open to new ideas. The more he learned about the teachings of Siddhartha Gautama, the more committed he became. The Four Noble Truths made perfect sense, and from then on he talked about the Eightfold Path to enlightenment and the end of attachments, delusions, and their consequent suffering.

Steve found another form of enlightenment during a short visit to England. A cousin took him sailing for the first time, and he was instantly hooked. He loved the simple concept of wind and water, and the idea of making his boat go faster than the next person's boat by manipulating the wind appealed to his competitive nature. He felt that sailing fast was something the Buddha would understand, and rather unexpectedly Steve had discovered the next passion in his life.

In the early 1990s Simon was living near Washington, D.C. He had purchased a 27-foot sailboat, and out of the blue Steve joined him. "He was always just turning up," Simon remembered fondly. "At that time we called him the wandering sibling. We never knew when he would turn up next or where from. But when he did, he always had bloody good stories to tell." They lived aboard the small boat for a while, sailing it whenever they could, and Steve realized that he wanted to make sailing his profession. Returning to Australia, he moved to Sydney and enrolled in a series of courses. He was a quick learner and soon became a qualified instructor while also obtaining a Yachtmaster's license. According to Pat, "He took a job as the skipper of a boat that did corporate parties in Sydney Harbor and taught sailing for the local charter company school. He also raced every chance he could. It was racing that he really loved." When Simon moved to Jersey City and purchased *Escape*, Steve soon turned up at his companionway step.

I FIRST met Christian Pschorr on Captiva Island, near Ft. Myers, Florida, while on assignment to write an article about the Offshore Sailing School. As part of my research I subjected my two young daughters to a weekend on the water, and Christian was their instructor. A talented teacher, fine sailor, and skilled and thoughtful writer, he had also played a mean sax in New York City jazz clubs in an earlier incarnation. Our paths kept crossing, and each time we met he supplied more information and more insight into Steve. They'd worked together for more than a year and spent many nights at the Lightship Restaurant bar. When I sailed into Newport, Rhode Island, a few summers later, I found Christian's black schooner—the successor to his 29-foot sloop—at anchor in the harbor. His charming wife, Michelle, and their two boys often looked after my boat as I returned periodically to work in Florida. Christian now delivers boats and runs an offshore training passage business, and we see each other at boat shows around the country.

Christian confirmed that Steve loved to race. "We all loved to race; the racing classes were the most fun. Better yet were those rare times when we raced without students, just the instructors. Unfortunately, Steve preferred to steer rather than better his sail-handling skills. He wielded the tiller like a base-ball bat. When Steve was at the helm we didn't win, but we had fun." Christian also said that Steve had a difficult time accepting responsibility for his mistakes and would blame his students for fender benders that resulted in broken rubrails and fiberglass gouges. "Don't get me wrong, though, he was a good instructor, knowledgeable and funny, just a bit clumsy at times. He claimed to be a Buddhist, and while I don't think he was devout, he certainly was patient, and that's important when teaching New Yorkers to sail."

In the autumn of 1998, with Simon preparing to set sail for a late-season crossing to England, the first stop on a circuitous journey to Australia, Steve was out of a home, so he accepted a job for the winter teaching at Colgate's Tortola branch in the British Virgin Islands. This was a common practice for Offshore Sailing School instructors. Simon had originally wanted to head south to the Caribbean, but Steve convinced him that it was foolhardy to sail into the tropics during the heart of the fall hurricane season. Simon decided to head across the Atlantic instead, a bold decision and probably just as risky as heading south. Unfortunately his passage didn't go well; he ran headlong into a gale off the Grand Banks and ended up being towed into Halifax, Nova Scotia, by the U.S. Coast Guard. He eventually returned to Liberty Landing to lick his wounds and try again the next year. Meanwhile, down in the islands, Steve had some bad luck of his own.

The school offered seven- and ten-day liveaboard cruising courses for students with varying degrees of experience. These popular classes gave new sailors a taste of the cruising lifestyle before they committed to buying a large, expensive, demanding boat. Steve was the skipper/instructor for one of these courses, and things went all wrong.

"Steve was a great guy," explains Tyler Pierce, who was the Offshore Sailing School's director of education and responsible for all the branch operations. "He was a little bit unorthodox, and he was a Buddhist, but that served him well. He didn't let little things bother him." Pierce explained the events that led to Steve putting a boat on the rocks. "One of the destinations for our boats on the liveaboard cruising course is a small cove on the back side of Marina Cay, just off Tortola. It's a little tricky getting in and out of the anchorage. Steve was following another boat and not watching the reef, and he drifted out of the pass. Next thing he knew he was on the rocks."

Steve managed to get all the students safely off the boat, and the boat was later salvaged. "Typically, an accident like that would be plenty of reason to fire an instructor," Pierce told me. "But Steve did the right thing. He didn't blame the skipper of the other boat; he took full responsibility. I was impressed and decided to give him another chance."

"His Buddhist conscience served him well," Christian Pschorr explained. "I was proud of the way he handled himself after the wreck. It was a turning point. He didn't blame someone else for his mistake. He acted like a skipper, like a captain for the first time. He was always a good sailor, and he was a good man too."

The winter in the islands did have its good side. Steve met Julia Henick, a lawyer from New York City and an aspiring sailor. Julia was one of his students, and soon she was more than an aspiring sailor and more than a student. They fell madly, wildly, completely in love. "Steve was truly smitten," Simon said later. "He was just crazy in love with Julia." Christian was skeptical at first, because Steve had told him on plenty of occasions that he was "no one woman's man," but it became clear that this was something different. Their romance was a whirlwind. Julia lived in Manhattan, not far from Liberty

Landing, and their affair lost no steam when Steve returned after the season in Tortola. He soon proposed, and they were married on May 29, 1999. Steve was 41.

"Julia was the best thing that ever happened to Steve," Simon reported. "She put solid direction in his life for the first time. She also cleaned him up a bit, you know? She bought him some decent clothes, had his teeth fixed, he even got an expensive haircut. He looked quite smart and he was happy about all of it. It was hard for some of the family to understand just how much he loved that woman."

During the winter Steve had read Derek Lundy's bestseller *Godforsaken Sea*, a taut narrative about the 1996–97 Vendée Globe race, one of the most disastrous and heroic yacht races ever sailed. Steve was captivated by Lundy's description of how fifteen entrants, each sailing solo in a 60-foot high-octane boat, set off on a nonstop race around the world. The race, which begins and ends at Les Sables-d'Olonne, France, is a grueling test of seamanship. The 1996–97 version was jinxed from the start, as the fleet ran into fierce gales in the Bay of Biscay and several boats retired. Later, in the wilderness of the Southern Ocean, that vast stretch of wind-driven mayhem below the 40th parallel, things turned deadly. Lundy described how Italian sailor Raphaël Dinelli's boat was capsized by a monstrous wave. Dinelli was miraculously rescued by a competitor, Englishman Pete Goss. Two other boats also capsized, and the Australian Coast Guard dramatically rescued the solo sailors. But in the saddest story of all, race headquarters lost communication with Canadian Gerry Roufs. Although four of his fellow competitors searched for him, it wasn't until the wreck of his boat washed up on the distant coast of Chile six months later that his death was confirmed.

Steve craved physical challenges and had been flirting with the idea of racing professionally. By the winter of 1998 he had decided that sailing was his future, but only after an ill-fated climbing expedition in the Andes the winter before. "He had ideas of climbing professionally, but he suffered from altitude sickness for the first time in his life," Tyler Pierce explained. "He decided to concentrate on sailing." Every page of Lundy's book inspired and terrified him, and when he finished reading it he was convinced that he wanted to join the elite ranks of sailors who race through the most dangerous waters on the planet. And he wanted to sail alone. How better to unite his two fundamental impulses—a fierce competitive drive and the pursuit of the Buddha's vision of enlightenment—than by driving a boat at top speed, by himself, thousands of miles from the nearest land? If life means suffering, and if the origin of suffering is attachment to the transient things of the world, how better to refute those attachments than in a small boat at sea? How better to follow the middle way toward enlightenment—neither self-indulgent nor self-mortifying—than alone at sea, utterly self-reliant? And where better to contemplate the fundamental truth that, for all our becoming, each of us is merely a nebula of atoms in a universe that is itself endlessly becoming?

When Steve Rigby celebrated his forty-second birthday two weeks after his wedding, he was immensely happy. He was healthy, handsome, in love, and brimming with confidence, and he had a plan. He was going to become a professional singlehanded sailor, and he was going to be good—maybe even a champion.

Dreams are only fantasies until they're propelled by a plan. Steve's dream of racing a million-dollar 60-foot sailboat around the world needed a starting point, a concrete transition from pushing a 26-foot daysailer around New York Harbor with a crew of pale stock traders. He needed a way to cut his teeth in the world of ocean racing, a venue that he and Julia could afford, and he found it in the Mini class.

Minis, formally called Transat 650s, are ridiculously small but incredibly fast boats designed for singlehanded ocean racing. The "650" refers to their metric length overall, 650 centimeters, which translates into less than 22 feet, and "Transat" means just what it implies, transatlantic. A devoted band of adventure seekers race these ultralight glorified surfboards across the Atlantic every other year in one of the most demanding sailing events on the planet. Between transatlantic races, a series of regattas is held across Europe each summer. While the Mini class has never been a success in North America, it is wildly popular in Europe, particularly in France and England. In Europe, Minis are to singlehanded sailing what carting is to Formula 1 motor racing—a training ground for superstars. Top Mini sailors become skippers in prestigious, big-money, big-sponsorship events like the Vendée Globe. Indeed, most top European Mini sailors are able to secure their corporate sponsors before making the jump to big boats.

Steve set his sights on the Mini class. First he would need to find a boat to buy, then he'd learn to sail it. His timing was perfect. The 1999 Mini Transat race was set to leave Concarneau, France, in late September. After a brief stop in the Canary Islands, the fleet would continue across the Atlantic. The lead boats would start turning up in Guadeloupe in early November, and Steve knew that a number of the finishers—having endured an ocean crossing in a bucking, spartan, skittish 21-footer—would be ready to sell their boats. His plan was to greet the fleet in Guadeloupe and sail away in a Mini of his own. He'd sail the boat in the Caribbean during the winter, then ship it to Europe in the spring to be ready for the 2000 Mini season.

He followed the race closely, and during the first leg he contacted the father of one of the racers.

"Steve phoned up my dad while I was holding on for dear life in the Bay of Biscay," Alex Bennett said with a laugh. "If he could have seen what I was going through right then, I don't think he'd have wanted to buy my boat." Alex was just 23 years old during the 1999 race but was already a rising star in professional racing circles.

"I had planned to sell my boat after the race anyway, so I was interested to hear about Steve's plans. I didn't meet up with him until I arrived in Guadeloupe, and by that time he had pretty well worked out the deal with my dad."

Just getting to Guadeloupe proved challenging for Bennett. The 1999 Mini Transat was one of the roughest on record.

"The first leg was a horror show, really," Bennett said. "We had 50 knots of wind on the second day out. One sailor had to be airlifted off his boat. Naturally the wind was coming from the southwest, which is the direction we wanted to go, and Minis are not made for going upwind."

During the height of the storm Bennett reduced his sails to the size of pillowcases, flying a storm jib and a trysail, which is a storm mainsail reserved for survival conditions. "Even with those tiny sails up I was getting rocked."

When he finally struggled into Lanzarote in the Canary Islands, Alex and his boat, *English Braids*, were in good shape. He stood in third place in a fleet of nearly forty boats and hoped to make up ground on the next leg. On October 22, 1999, Bennett and the others set off on leg two, the nearly

3,000-mile passage to Guadeloupe. *English Braids*, named after Alex's sponsor, a UK cordage company, took off like a rocket and was among the leaders early on. "For some reason, the French got the name wrong," Bennett said. "They assumed it should be *English Breads*, not *Braids*, and that stuck. All the press reported that I was on *English Breads*."

Bennett's hopes for winning the race suffered a blow when his autopilot failed, and he was forced to steer by hand. When he reached the point of exhaustion, he would have to take the sails down long enough to get a short nap. Then he'd do it again. "It's impossible to keep up when you have to stop to sleep. It was very frustrating. I steered as long as I could, but you do have to sleep sometimes. The way you win Mini races is to make the boat sail fast, but also to have it self-steer so it can keep moving while you're resting."

Bennett pushed *English Braids* to the limits of his endurance. "We touched 20 knots sometimes. Of course, everything has to be spot on, but when it is, you can really haul the mail. But you have to be right on top of it too, because you can wipe out. I was able to sustain this kind of high-alert sailing for 2, maybe 3 hours max, then your nerves are fried." Despite the failure of his autopilot, Bennett made a fast passage and finished fifth overall in a strong fleet.

"I was disappointed with my place—I knew I could have done better—but that's the luck of ocean racing, isn't it? I was just happy to be across. The Mini Transat is really a tough race. I was ready for a different kind of sailing. It was time for *English Braids* to have a new owner. I was ready to turn her over to Steve, and wished him well with the boat. You could see the hunger in his eyes. He seemed like he was well suited for Mini sailing."

MARIGOT

"Besides the art of sailing, the sense of pride—the intimate
relationship of an individual to his ship—has much to do
with happy voyages. Well planned and executed passages are
rarely spectacular. Most exciting experiences are the result
of error—which of course can happen to anyone. But the
spectacular tales are, more often than not, the result of
poor planning, inadequate equipment or poor seamanship."

Charles Borden, *Sea Quest*

In 1981, Marigot was my first exotic port of call. After
an uneventful five-day passage from Bermuda, St. Martin loomed
on the horizon, its rolling hills hunched like a protective big
brother over low-slung Anguilla. My crew and I tacked through
late afternoon shadows under the hills, thrilled to have reached
the Caribbean islands. Slipping through an armada of anchored
boats, we dropped the hook off a restaurant named La Vie en
Rose, which is still there today. In those days La Vie en Rose was
the cornerstone of Marigot's colorful waterfront. We spent some
memorable evenings in the bar downstairs. Each night before
closing time the sound system blasted Edith Piaf's legendary
recording of "La Vie en Rose," and we sang along in brutal
French, toasting one another with cheap Bordeaux. I related this
story to Carl when he told me what he planned to name his boat.
At first I thought he would cry, but then his eyes lit up and he
shook his head at the mysterious workings of the universe.

In the early 1980s Marigot was a spicy stew of West Indian and French cultures. The town was small, but the wharf bustled with sailboats and local craft. The outdoor market sold vegetables, not T-shirts, and the aromas that wafted across the harbor stirred the senses. The women were the most beautiful I had ever seen, dark skinned, fair eyed, and completely put together as only French women can be. We would dinghy in for baguettes and fresh fruit each morning. The harbor was crowded with hard-core cruisers and graceful wooden charter boats. We lingered there for weeks.

Marigot was the adopted home of Guillaume Llobregat. His father, Jean Jacques Llobregat, had discovered the island when he picked it out of the blue for a family holiday in 1978.

"St. Martin? We had never heard of St. Martin," Guillaume's sister, Camille, remembers. "We wanted to go to Martinique or Guadeloupe."

The family was living in Toulouse, in southwestern France, where the senior Llobregat was making a transition from high school history teacher to entrepreneur. The family fell in love with the island, which is half Dutch and half French, an incongruous but harmonious arrangement that could only work in the Caribbean. Jean Jacques sensed opportunity on the sleepy island. He began investing in real estate, and by 1990 the island was home base for the entire Llobregat clan. Those many trips to St. Martin were ideal for young Guillaume, for his life revolved around water sports. He was, according to his sister, "addicted to water."

Guillaume had been born in Toulouse in 1963. As a boy he watched barges transit the Canal du Midi and longed to hitch a ride and follow them to the sea. "He was interested in boats and sailing from an early age," says his mother, Jacquelyn. "It was all sailing, sailing, sailing. He had pictures of sailboats on his bedroom walls." He learned to sail during summer holidays at the coast, and at age 18 he enrolled in the famous Les Glénans Sailing School in Brittany. Operating since 1947, the Glénans School is the largest in Europe, with locations all over France. Their course manual, which has been published in many languages, is in its sixth edition, with hundreds of thousands of copies in print. Glénans courses have always emphasized that sailing is more than a technique to be acquired; it is also a tool to help the sailor understand the sea and himself. Sailing, the school teaches, is a natural extension of living. Guillaume thrived at Glénans, completing all three levels of training before going on to qualify as an instructor at the school. He later earned a captain's license with a commercial rating. He knew what he wanted to do with his life—he wanted to sail.

Jean Jacques Llobregat had been born in French Morocco before making his way to Toulouse as a young man. The name Llobregat, however, is Catalonian. Catalonia, the northeast region of Spain, borders southwest France and the Mediterranean and maintains its own culture, language, and distinct identity. The Llobregat River, more a stream really, originates in the Pyrenees and flows to Barcelona, the Catalan capital, which is just a 3-hour drive from Toulouse.

"From Toulouse, Barcelona is the nearest major city. We are much more interested in Barcelona than Paris," Jean Jacques Llobregat explained. "There is really no comparison between the two cities." Once he was able to drive, Barcelona became a home away from home for young Guillaume. He was interested in architecture as well as sailing, and the sensuous, gravity-defying buildings designed by Antoni Gaudí intrigued him. On one of his trips to the city he met Alicia, and she intrigued him too.

"It was on Las Ramblas. I was having a coffee and Guillaume walked by. It was love at first sight," Alicia says, without a trace of embarrassment. "We were young, but we shared dreams of sailing and traveling." Guillaume and Alicia were married in 1987, when they were both 24. Two years later they flew to the Grenadines, a jeweled necklace of islands between St. Vincent and Grenada in the Windward Islands of the southeast Caribbean. Their plan was to establish a Caribbean charter business, and they were in the market for a big but affordable boat.

From an ad in the classified section of *Bateaux*, Guillaume tracked down an attractively priced 65-foot staysail schooner named *Frederic-Anne*. The ferrocement schooner, which had been built near the Glénans School on the rugged coast of Brittany, operated out of Union Island, the southernmost of the Grenadines. Union Island's verdant peaks and reef-fringed harbors have earned it the title of "the Tahiti of the Caribbean," and its majesty overwhelmed Guillaume. He stubbed his cigarette in the sand and announced that the island was too beautiful for an ugly habit like smoking. He never smoked again.

They found *Frederic-Anne* moored in Clifton Harbor. After a bit of haggling they agreed to a price, and after a survey and sea trial—and after Jean Jacques wired a little more money— Guillaume and Alicia became the owners of the schooner. At age 26 Guillaume Llobregat was master of his own ship and his own fate. What could be better than being young, in love, and the owner of a classic sailing ship?

Union Island has long been a popular base for day charter vessels. Most of the well-known Caribbean schooners and big ketches have worked the turquoise waters of Clifton Harbor and nearby Palm Island at one time or another. With so much competition, Guillaume and Alicia struggled at first, but soon they built a respectable business. By this time the Llobregat family had left Toulouse for good, relocating to St. Martin, and Jean Jacques convinced Guillaume and Alicia to relocate there as well. He assured his son that the charter opportunities in Marigot were untapped. In the summer of 1990, prior to making the passage to St. Martin, Guillaume sailed *Frederic-Anne* to Puerto La Cruz, Venezuela, for a refit, taking advantage of the cheap labor and materials there to have the boat completely upgraded and repainted.

Ferrocement construction is a controversial way of building a boat. Some sailors swear by it, but most swear at it. A ferrocement hull is formed by troweling concrete onto a steel wire frame, layer by layer. The process dates back to the 1850s in France and has always been an economical way to build boats. Because no special tools or molds are required, it has also been popular with amateur builders, and many ferrocement boats were slapped together in California fields in the 1960s and '70s. This was the golden age of cruising, when the voyage mattered more than the boat. A small but dedicated band of hippie cruisers set off in some of the ugliest and most unseaworthy hulks ever to ply the high seas. This armada of penniless cruisers did little to enhance the reputation of ferrocement boats.

Frederic-Anne was a different breed, professionally built. From a distance, her fair hull had the mirror-smooth finish of fiberglass. She had traditional lines with a sweeping sheer—the curve of her deck in profile—and a pronounced bowsprit. Fitted out with modern gear and top-quality hardware, she was no "character" boat designed for tacky sunset harbor cruises. She was an oceangoing boat.

Her black masts were of anodized aluminum to match the black hull. No boat is lovelier than a well-apportioned and well-kept staysail schooner with all canvas flying, and *Frederic-Anne* could carry all her canvas comfortably in far windier conditions than most other boats. She was made for the stiff and steady trade winds that wash the Caribbean.

After the refit, Guillaume singlehanded *Frederic-Anne* to St. Martin, a 500-mile nonstop passage from Venezuela. Singlehanding a boat like *La Vie en Rose* or *English Braids* is one thing, but handling a 65-foot, 75-ton staysail schooner is another. It takes skill, strength, cunning, and nerves of steel.

When Guillaume arrived in Marigot, he and Alicia immediately set up a day charter operation, taking tourists from the public wharf to Cove Bay, 6 miles from Marigot on the island of Anguilla. There Llobregat and his mate, usually Jacques Santos after 1997, would ferry the guests ashore to lounge on one of the best beaches in the world or to snorkel along the rocks that stretched off the eastern corner of the bay. Llobregat and Santos would serve lunch aboard and then sail back to Marigot. *Frederic-Anne* was licensed to carry up to twenty-five passengers, and many days she was full. After discharging his passengers, Llobregat would anchor *Frederic-Anne* in the outer harbor. Sometimes he made his way to La Vie en Rose for a drink before heading home.

By 1999, St. Martin looked more like Cancún than the sleepy island of 1981. The Dutch side of the island was one huge construction project, with half-finished hotels, condos, marinas, and commercial buildings lining the traffic-snarled road from Philipsburg to Simpson Bay. Tourist sprawl had been better controlled on the French side, but there too a bustle of commerce overlay the island's former charm, and elegant shops and cafés reached many blocks inland. La Vie en Rose still held down a piece of prime real estate, but it was just one of many restaurants lining the Marigot quay.

A few miles outside Marigot, the Llobregat family compound sat on a hill in the Lowlands, overlooking the sea. This section of St. Martin was not all low-lying land, but it was, for the most part, affluent, and it was also beautiful. The family home was visible to port, high above the golden sands of Long Beach, as Guillaume Llobregat steered *Frederic-Anne* around the western edge of St. Martin on the morning of November 15, 1999. A handsome man with curly dark hair, Guillaume was over 6 feet tall, lean and strong. He looked like a man who could haul up *Frederic-Anne*'s huge mainsail by himself. While Jacques Santos busied himself trimming the sails and securing all the loose items on deck, Guillaume continued to evaluate his options.

Leaving the house that morning, he had told Alicia that he was going to sail south until Lenny ran its course. When the coast was clear, he'd sail back. It might be days before he could return, he told her. He said he'd try to maintain contact with Radio Martinique and relay periodic reports of his progress. He reassured his wife that he was making the right decision and that he loved her.

But something about this wrong-way hurricane that was forcing a delay in his charter season was galling Llobregat, and now he was reconsidering his decision to head south. He was weighing an even riskier option.

NOVEMBER 15

"He always thought of the sea as la mar, what people call her in Spanish when they love her. Sometimes those who love her say bad things of her but they are always said as though she were a woman. Some of the younger fishermen spoke of her as el mar, which is masculine. They spoke of her as a contestant or a place or even as an enemy. But the old man always thought of her as feminine and as something that gave or withheld great favors, and if she did wild or wicked things it was because she could not help them."

Ernest Hemingway, *The Old Man and the Sea*

On Monday morning, November 15, 1999, Carl rummaged through the collection of charts he kept in a small hammock above the navigation desk, searching for National Imagery and Mapping Agency Chart No. W402, the Caribbean Sea. This mundane task, like so many others, requires a disproportionate expenditure of energy on a small boat at sea. Several times each day a singlehander asks himself whether a sail change or maintenance chore or hot meal is really worth the effort. One after another chart refused to remain unrolled long enough to give Carl a good look at it, but he finally found the one he was looking for and spread it across the saloon table. Holding the huge chart in place with heavy books on each corner, he beseeched *La Vie en Rose* to hold steady a few minutes so that he could study it.

The entire Caribbean is a big area to show on one chart, even a large one. Chart No. 402 ranges from the tip of Cuba and Panama in the west to the Venezuelan coast, Trinidad, and the Windward and Leeward islands in the east, more than 30 degrees of longitude and 14 degrees or 840 nautical miles of latitude. To cover such a vast area the chart employs a very small scale—2,750,000:1—meaning that 1 inch on the chart represents 2,750,000 inches, almost 38 nautical miles, on the earth's surface. In its northeast quadrant the chart shows the waters north of Puerto Rico and the Virgin Islands where *La Vie en Rose* was poised to make her entry into the Caribbean Sea.

A dutiful navigator by habit, Carl transferred his position—approximately 20° north and 64.5° west—onto the new chart, using dividers to pick the coordinates off the chart's margins and a pencil to mark the spot. Despite his anxiety about Hurricane Lenny, he felt a passagemaker's familiar sense of accomplishment at the transition from one chart to the next, and he may also have been intrigued to see that he was just 100 miles or so north of the Puerto Rican Deep. This sliver of an underwater canyon reaches down to 30,000 feet in places, making it the deepest spot in the Atlantic and one of the deepest pockets of ocean anywhere on the planet. Carl had a penchant for the macabre, and he may well have thought to himself that the Puerto Rican Deep would be a terrible place to sink. Perhaps he even morbidly wondered how long it would take *La Vie* to reach the bottom. After noting his position, he took his time carefully plotting Lenny's latest coordinates. As of 0800 Atlantic Standard Time, Lenny's eye was at 15.1° north latitude and 76.4° west longitude, about 160 miles south of Kingston, Jamaica. As the petrel flies, the eye was more than 700 miles west-southwest of *La Vie en Rose*.

The visual picture was reassuring. Although the local wind had fallen during the night and shifted to the south, dramatically slowing *La Vie*'s progress, the Category 2 storm was still a long way away—16 inches across the chart from Carl's current position. The forecast called for the storm to meander east while gaining some strength for at least another day or day and a half before turning northeast and eventually north. At its current forward speed of 8 miles per hour, or less than 7 knots—about 170 nautical miles in 24 hours—Lenny was unlikely to impact Carl before he was safely in port, and if the track curved north as predicted, the storm would pass to his west and not affect him at all.

But Carl knew that you can't trust hurricanes to do what they're supposed to do. What if the storm found its footing and sped up? And just exactly where was Lenny heading, anyway? There was plenty of uncertainty associated with the forecast, especially beyond the 24-hour horizon. Hurricanes typically travel at a rate of 8 to 14 knots, and predicting the forward speed of a storm is the most challenging aspect of hurricane forecasting.

Carl listened to every forecast update he could tune in. Perfect Paul became like another crew member aboard. The High Seas Forecast for the Caribbean Sea and the southwestern North Atlantic was broadcast on several single-sideband frequencies at 0330, 0500, 0930, 1130, 1600, 1730, and 2200 hours UTC—or 4 hours earlier in Atlantic Standard Time. In addition to these official forecasts, at 1700 AST, or 5 P.M., Carl hung on the words of other cruisers, also en route to the islands, who were getting advice from Herb Hilgenberg. Hilgenberg was operating a daily weather net for Atlantic sailors under the well-known call sign of Southbound II, and he was worried about a large low-pressure trough east of the Leeward Islands that seemed poised to move south. He felt it was quite possible that this low would converge with Lenny, which would both add to Lenny's strength and keep it plowing eastward rather than curving north.

At the National Hurricane Center in Miami, Florida, nine different models were being used to predict Lenny's future track, and four others were attempting to forecast the storm's future intensity. Of the track models, a couple showed Lenny turning left to slice through the Mona Passage between Hispaniola and Puerto Rico, then curving west to whip into the southern Bahamas. A couple of others had Lenny arcing more slowly to the northeast, scoring a direct hit on Puerto Rico, before curving to the north. And a few others predicted that Lenny would continue eastward with just a slow drift to the north and rock the Virgin Islands as it passed by. Most models showed that an upper-level ridge of high pressure would eventually deflect Lenny to the northeast and then to the north. The disagreement was on when this would happen.

The official forecast averaged the models into a track that continued east for a day or so before turning northeast to hit Puerto Rico. The heart of St. Thomas is a mere 40 miles east of Puerto Rico. Island residents were urged to make immediate preparations. At 1700 Atlantic Standard Time, all of Puerto Rico and the U.S. and British Virgin Islands were put under a hurricane watch, meaning that hurricane conditions were possible within 36 hours.

By late afternoon, *La Vie en Rose* was perched below the 20th parallel, still in the Atlantic but almost close enough to the tropical islands of the Caribbean for Carl to smell them. She had made slow progress through the previous night and during the day as the winds veered gradually from east to south. According to the November pilot chart for the Caribbean, a guide for predicting general climatic conditions, the likelihood of *La Vie en Rose* encountering southerly winds was less than 1 in 10. The southerlies this day were a precursor of Lenny's approach.

Roughly 100 miles from his destination, Charlotte Amalie Harbor on St. Thomas, Carl pondered his next move. *La Vie*'s forward speed had dropped to around 4 or 5 knots as she punched into choppy seas in a moderate 10- to 15-knot wind. What was worse, with the wind from the south, Carl was forced to tack back and forth across the wind, and this zigzag course required 1½ miles of sailing for every mile of southward progress. Tacking meant that it would take longer to reach St. Thomas, as long as 35 to 40 hours if existing conditions held. That was cutting things too close, especially given the thought of making the final approach to the south-facing harbor entrance in building winds and seas along a treacherous lee shore.

Carl may have briefly considered dropping his sails and motoring directly toward the island, but he knew that with his small 40-horsepower Volvo diesel he wouldn't make much speed, especially because the seas seemed to be building—a harbinger of strengthening winds. *La Vie en Rose* was designed to sail, not to power efficiently against a head sea. He knew that he might not have enough fuel to motor all the way in, and if he used up his reserve in a futile attempt to push against the wind and seas, his options would be severely reduced when the time came to make landfall. *La Vie en Rose* carried 50 gallons of fuel in a stainless steel tank and a 10-gallon emergency reserve in two plastic jerry cans lashed on deck. The engine burned approximately ¾ gallon of fuel per hour of running time. For the most part Carl ran the engine only when he had to, for an hour or so in the morning and then again in the early evening to charge the batteries. This kept the lights, radios, fridge, and autopilot running. But he had reluctantly motored during some calms earlier in the passage and had already used about half his fuel.

Sometime in the afternoon of November 15, Carl made a fateful decision. Having concluded that a series of short tacks offered no reasonable assurance of getting him into Charlotte Amalie comfortably ahead of the storm, he put *La Vie en Rose* on starboard tack and bore away to the southeast. Assuming— as sailors must do—that the Hurricane Center was right, the eye of the storm was on track to pass close to the west of his current position, bringing hurricane-strength winds right over-head. It was essential for Carl to be somewhere else by then, and his new heading would accomplish that. It would carry him well east of Charlotte Amalie, but the opposite tack would have taken him southwest, directly toward the storm. He might also have considered fleeing west or north, but in those directions, too, the storm could have tracked him down. Heading east would put even more distance between *La Vie* and Lenny when the fickle storm finally turned north and started acting like a proper Caribbean hurricane.

La Vie en Rose liked her new course, and by opening the angle between the wind and the sails, Carl was able to boost her speed appreciably. On a similar close reach in the Keys, Carl and I had once galloped along at more than 6 knots. Carl no doubt eased out the main and the jib a few inches until they were drawing smartly, and the added draft translated directly into horsepower. He had probably rolled in his big genoa during the night and was down to his smaller working jib, a flat-cut sail designed for upwind sailing. His new course aimed *La Vie* at the northern Leeward Islands of Anguilla and St. Martin and offered a reasonable chance of outflanking Lenny completely. With a bit of luck, as the storm moved north, his wind would clock into the southwest, allowing him to fetch the British Virgin Islands. There were plenty of safe harbors in the BVIs, not to mention a few nice beach bars, and Carl remembered them well from his days of sailing with Tom Criste. Those were familiar waters, and Carl always gravitated toward the familiar. And if Lenny tracked east longer than predicted, he still had the option of fleeing directly east, out into the Atlantic. Once Lenny was no longer a threat, he'd sail back to St. Thomas. He had a plan, and that in itself was invigorating.

Steve Rigby must have been extremely frustrated by the lack of wind. Some 230 miles southeast of where Carl Wake on *La Vie en Rose* was experiencing moderate southerlies, Rigby and *English Braids* languished in calm, hot, humid conditions. What was worse, the annoying zephyrs were blowing from the direction toward which Steve wanted to sail, the northwest. A long, low swell rolled the tiny boat from side to side, causing the carefully collected wind to spill from the slatting sails. This was maddening sailing, not at all what Rigby had anticipated when he cleared Basse-Terre, Guadeloupe, the night before.

Mini 650s are designed for blazing off-the-wind performance but are not terribly efficient sailing upwind. "They're pigs to weather," Alex Bennett, the British sailor who raced *English Braids* across the Atlantic, says. It's a matter of hydrodynamics. The Mini's flat, flared hull shape encourages easy surfing when sailing before the wind, adding the forward speed of the wave to the boat's speed to create thrilling and occasionally out-of-control sailing. When beating against the wind, however, the boat is firmly rooted to the water and held in check by the forces of gravity and friction. Speed, for the most part, then becomes a function of waterline length. More specifically, a keelboat's theoretical hull speed—the top speed it can attain without surfing or planing—is dictated by a simple formula: the square root of the waterline length multiplied by 1.34.

For *English Braids* this translated into 6 knots under ideal conditions, and the conditions Steve Rigby was experiencing were far from ideal. With little or no wind and a jumbled sea, *English Braids* was drifting along at 2 or 3 knots. This slow pace, equal to that of an overweight, out-of-shape baby boomer strolling through a shopping mall, was still pretty impressive. As Steve Maseda, an experienced small-boat racer and past president of the class association for the Melges 24, a lightweight rocket ship of a sailboat similar to the Mini, explains, "When you can sail upwind at half the speed of the wind in a small boat, you're doing better than okay, you are working the boat." Rigby was used to light airs from sailing in New York Harbor, and he was skilled at coaxing the most from a boat under those circumstances. A competitive sailor by nature and ambition, he was tweaking the sails to keep *English Braids* moving.

Although he reminded himself that he wasn't in a hurry, these were conditions to try even a Buddhist's soul. They were also rare for mid-November in the Caribbean Sea. The lack of wind was caused by a low-pressure system hovering east of the northern Leeward Islands and by Lenny building in the west. Steve was right between the two systems. This persistent low—the very one Herb Hilgenberg feared would couple with Lenny—was primarily responsible for disrupting the normal trade wind flow over the Caribbean basin south and east of the Virgin Islands.

Steve was surely aware that the barometer was falling, although at his position, 40 miles or so west of the island of Montserrat, it had not started to freefall. That unnerving plummet was still a day away. As an Offshore Sailing School instructor, he also knew about Buys Ballot's Law. This simple observation determines the direction toward the center of a nearby low-pressure system. If you're in the Northern Hemisphere with your back to the wind, you'll find the center of the low over your left shoulder. Using this method, Steve could have inferred something of the low hovering east of St. Martin, and he may also have associated the heavy westerly swell, which churned steadily below the light chop rippling across the surface, as a sign that a major storm was approaching from the west. Like the south winds experienced by *La Vie en Rose* to the north, the swell passing under *English Braids*'s deep keel was a murmured warning.

But Steve was both preoccupied and out of touch. Without a functioning autopilot, he was a slave to the helm, and his only option for hearing weather reports was his VHF radio. He was well beyond the radio's 10- to 15-mile receiving range, and anyway the forecasts in those waters would have been in French.

A LIGHT northwesterly, the same wind that was plaguing Steve Rigby in his engineless Mini 650, allowed Guillaume Llobregat and Jacques Santos to make good progress under sail and engine power as they sped away from Marigot Harbor during the late morning hours of November 15. After plotting Lenny's latest position and listening to the forecast, Llobregat shaped a course that would take them west of Saba Island. Earlier he had planned to sail due south, but now he sailed southwest instead. Like almost every other observer, he assumed that Lenny would eventually track to the northeast, leaving *Frederic-Anne* well below the main thrust of the storm but still not too far from home. Llobregat hoped to return to St. Martin as quickly as possible once the storm passed. He wanted to make sure his family was safe and to assist with any cleanup or repairs at the Llobregat family compound in the Lowlands. He worried about Alicia, knowing that tropical storms terrified her. She was from Spain, and there were no hurricanes in the Mediterranean. Finally, too, he needed to get his charter season going as quickly as possible. He needed some positive cash flow in the wake of his refit at Bobby's Marina.

Jacques Santos was busy lashing everything on deck that might possibly blow away and stowing loose items such as boathooks and cockpit cushions. "He was always working when he was on the boat," Alicia says. "He never sat still." Although *Frederic-Anne* was a strong and seaworthy vessel, she was not an ideal boat in which to weather a serious blow at sea. She was cumbersome to handle and wasn't rigged for survival conditions. Few boats are, but she had a couple of design features that made her particularly vulnerable.

The large portlights, or windows, in her cabin trunk were one weak point for any breaking waves crashing aboard, and there were also several large wooden hatches on her foredeck. These deck openings provided excellent ventilation when anchored off Anguilla during a day charter, but they were a hazard at sea. If they failed, they would allow ocean water to cascade below. Santos made sure they were dogged down tight. He had great confidence in Captain Guillaume, and he wasn't especially worried. Llobregat had told him that they were just being cautious, that he had every intention of avoiding the storm, and that they'd soon be back in Marigot having a drink at La Vie en Rose. Santos was worried mainly about his wife. He'd been married only a few months, and he wondered where she would seek shelter if Lenny hit St. Martin after all.

Guillaume Llobregat was a professional sailor, well schooled in the dynamics of hurricanes. You don't operate a charter business in the Caribbean without understanding the dos and don'ts of tropical revolving storms. He recognized that the deep, undulating swell traveling from west to east was Lenny's forerunner. He knew too that hurricanes are divided into halves, or semicircles: a dangerous semicircle and a navigable one. "Navigable" in this context is a Panglossian misnomer if ever there was one. More accurately stated, it is the slightly less dangerous side of an almost unimaginable nightmare.

In the Northern Hemisphere, the dangerous semicircle is always the right half of the storm with respect to its direction of travel. The semicircles can be further divided into quarters, and of the four pieces in the resultant storm "pie," the most dangerous is the leading right-hand quadrant. There the forward speed of the storm is added to its embedded wind speeds, making the winds even more intense. What makes this quadrant especially deadly, however, is that the rotation of its winds draws a vessel into the vortex, toward the eye of the storm. Conversely, within the left, or so-called navigable, side of a hurricane, the trailing quadrant offers the best hope for survival in a small vessel. There the storm's forward motion lessens its embedded wind speeds, and a boat is more apt to be spat out than pulled in by a retreating storm.

Most Atlantic hurricanes travel in a west or northwest direction before bending toward the north and finally to the northeast. This time-tested behavior is ingrained in the consciousness not just of mariners but of all coastal dwellers from Central America to Nova Scotia. Since the mid-1990s a record number of hurricanes has assaulted the U.S. mainland, and experts predict the trend will continue. Hurricanes are made-for-television events. They unfold slowly, the plots twist and turn while they draw closer to our shores, and the story often ends in a photogenic climax as they crash ashore with a vengeance. From June through November, those of us who live in Hurricane Alley regularly tune in to the Weather Channel for the latest tropical update. Tracking storm systems becomes part of the daily routine. Schoolkids from Louisiana to North Carolina learn the meaning of latitude and longitude while plotting storm coordinates on maps donated by local businesses.

The classic Atlantic hurricane, the so-called Cape Verde hurricane, first appears as a blip on a satellite image, a disorganized cluster of clouds thousands of miles away off the west coast of Africa. What begins as a harmattan, a hot, dry, dust-laden desert wind, stalls over the ocean, and a low-pressure system forms. As the low deepens, it begins a slow march across the tropical Atlantic, following what meteorologists call an African easterly wave, a mini, westward-traveling jet stream. Warm waters feed the system, and if it manages to avoid upper-level wind shear and marauding high-pressure systems that try to tear it apart, it eventually acquires a cyclonic, or counterclockwise, rotation. When these spiraling winds reach 34 knots the system is classified as a tropical storm, and at that point it is christened. The first storm of a season begins with "A," and later storms begin with successive letters of the alphabet. The names alternate between male and female, and short, distinctive names are favored—Lenny, for instance.

Once a storm has a name, it seems to acquire a personality. As it approaches the Caribbean islands its every move is scrutinized by a cadre of experts and dutifully reported to a nervous public. A drop in barometric pressure or a sharp increase in wind speed is like a spike in the cholesterol count of a heart patient; it might be critical, or it might mean nothing. At 50 minutes past the hour—or even more frequently as the storm draws closer—the Weather Channel flashes the familiar yellow cone, a three- or five-day outline of the storm's projected track. We all hope and pray that our island or stretch of coastline is not included in the dreaded yellow swath. Then the Weather Channel invariably cuts to a reporter standing on a beach. Clad in a baseball cap and rain jacket, she or he looks serious. She dismisses the teenagers with their surfboards in the background as reckless kids and instructs responsible adults to seize the moment to batten down the hatches. The scene then dissolves to a Home Depot store where people are frantically loading plywood, batteries, and portable generators onto shopping trolleys. Eventually, en route to a commercial break, we see canned footage of a lonely sailboat on a mooring, bucking to and fro, stoically awaiting the monster's arrival.

But not all hurricanes form off Africa and plod like foot soldiers across the ocean, especially not late-season storms. These "Johnny-come-latelies" spring to life on our side of the world, often in the western Caribbean. They suck up energy from waters that have been heated all summer to more than 80° Fahrenheit to depths in excess of 100 to 200 feet, and soon they are no longer limited to dumping buckets of rain on tropically depressed tourists and spawning occasional gusty winds that send colorful beach umbrellas pitchpoling onto hotel verandas. Two of the most destructive storms in recorded history—Mitch in 1998 and Katrina in 2005—roared to hurricane strength in the western Caribbean and the Gulf of Mexico, respectively.

But even these deadly storms almost always follow a predictable path. First they head west, gathering steam and terrifying folks from Belize to Cancún. Then they turn northwest

—through the Yucatán Straits, feeding on the warm waters of the Gulf Stream's feeder currents. Some, like Katrina, head north through the Gulf of Mexico and unleash their venom on low-lying coastal areas from Texas to the Florida Panhandle. Others, like Wilma, another 2005 record-breaking hurricane, angle northeast and shoot across the Florida Peninsula, reemerging in the Atlantic. From there, they typically speed up dramatically, skirt the Atlantic coast, and eventually disintegrate in cool North Atlantic waters.

Lenny wasn't following either of these well-rehearsed scripts. It was heading the wrong way, confounding not only the experts at the National Hurricane Center and the Weather Channel but experienced sailors too. Almost all of them assumed that the storm would turn north. It was very difficult to accept the notion that Lenny might continue tracking east. For mariners, the hidden danger in Lenny's easterly heading was that it fundamentally changed the normal disposition of the dangerous and navigable semicircles. Lefty Lenny packed its strongest winds not in its northwest quadrant like a westbound hurricane or its northeast quadrant like a northbound storm, but down in the southeast quadrant instead. In this case, the south side— normally the safer—was the side to stay away from at all costs.

Even if Lenny's meteorological sleight of hand had registered with Guillaume Llobregat or Carl Wake, it's unlikely that either man would have adjusted his tactics. They would still have clung to the belief that Lenny had to turn eventually. All hurricanes did, according to gospel, and their strategy for storm avoidance was almost certainly based on this. But tropical storms don't always turn north. Probably neither man remembered Hurricane Klaus, a sputtering storm that, like Lenny, formed near Jamaica and tracked east-northeast across the

Caribbean in 1984. Klaus didn't attain hurricane status until after it had passed Puerto Rico and disappeared into the Atlantic, and so inflicted little damage. It was easy to forget.

As the afternoon of November 15 wore on, there was suddenly hope that Lenny might be another Klaus after all. Earlier in the day, weather officer Lieutenant Colonel Roy Deatherage and the crew aboard the WC-130 Hurricane Hunter aircraft had set off for another firsthand look at Lenny, and the news was heartening. The storm was wobbling, coming apart at the seams, and the flight crew had trouble even finding the eye. It was not easily discernible with satellite imagery or with the onboard radar system. Lenny had lost steam and organization, and its maximum sustained winds were down to 75 knots. This weakening caught forecasters off guard, because the atmospheric conditions seemed favorable for the storm to intensify. Lenny was a difficult hurricane to get a handle on. Now it seemed that further weakening was a distinct possibility. Maybe it was just too late in the season to sustain a hurricane; maybe there simply wasn't enough heat in the water to a great enough depth to provide the necessary fuel. By the time the Hurricane Hunter touched down at Keesler Air Force Base in Biloxi, Lenny had been downgraded to Category 1 on the Saffir-Simpson scale.

This update, which was broadcast that evening on the High Seas Forecast and on every weather net in the Caribbean, was no doubt well received by the crews of *La Vie en Rose* and *Frederic-Anne*. Maybe Lenny would sputter and die, leaving behind nothing more than rain showers and an annoying swell. Aboard *English Braids*, however, it's doubtful that Steve Rigby even knew that Lenny existed on the calm evening of November 15, 1999. He wasn't cheering the news that the hurricane seemed to be losing power. He was slouched in the uncomfortable cockpit of his tiny boat, weary from more than 24 hours at the helm, whistling for wind.

The calms stretched over a wide area in the Caribbean, both on the water and on shore. Normally bustling Road Town on Tortola was quiet. November 15 was a holiday in the British Virgin Islands, and most businesses and shops were closed. According to Mark Henry, who lived aboard his 37-foot sloop *Recess* in Road Harbour during the fall of 1999, residents seemed split about the need to take Lenny seriously. "I had my storm anchors out, but other boaters hadn't even taken down their awnings. Some buildings were boarded up, but most were not."

There wasn't a breath of air in town. Local forecaster David Jones continued to issue stern warnings, asserting that although Lenny had lost a little strength, a restrengthening was not only possible but probable. He urged residents to take the storm seriously. The authorities, at least, were listening. The Office of Disaster Preparedness urged charter companies to recall their boats, and soon safe harbors all over the BVIs were brimming with anchored boats and unhappy charter crews. "I remember Lenny well," said Barney Crook, president of Tortola Marine Management. "It had us all confused, but the reports seemed to imply that Tortola and the Virgins in general were in for a blow. We made sure we had people ready to man the radio at Virgin Islands Search and Rescue." Airport officials strongly recommended that all private planes be flown off the island, and as of that evening they suspended commercial flights. The police and fire departments were put on alert.

These measures were a major inconvenience, but with Hurricane Jose fresh in their memories, island officials were not taking any chances.

HAVANA

"Every man needs to find a peak, a mountain top or a remote island of his own choosing that he reaches under his own power alone in his own good time."

Alain Gerbault, *In Quest of the Sun*

CALL me Eddie Pilot," our driver said in heavily accented English. "That's good enough." We were bound for La Floridita, the Havana bar made famous by Ernest Hemingway and by his second-favorite drink, the daiquiri. We had already been to the hole-in-the-wall bar nearby, La Bodeguita del Medio, where we drank a couple of his favorite, the sweet rum-and-mint concoctions called mojitos. We were doing our best to endure a forced vacation in Cuba. I had completed my magazine assignment earlier in the day, interviewing Papa's old boat captain Gregorio Fuentes. At age 102 he was remarkably lucid, and we had a pleasant chat at his home in the former fishing village of Cojímar. I had all I needed to write the article when I returned home after sailing to St. Thomas and celebrating Thanksgiving with Carl.

It was early evening, November 15, when Eddie dropped us off in the heart of the old city, promising to return later that night in his patched-up but immaculate, thirty-five-year-old, Russian-built Lada. Instead of sitting at the bar and nursing another drink, I had hoped to be loading provisions aboard and making final preparations for the passage to St. Thomas, but we weren't leaving anytime soon. Cuba was closed to anybody coming or going by boat until La Cumbre, the summit meeting of Latin American leaders, concluded. Fidel Castro had the power to seal off his country like a Ziploc bag, and police patrolled every street corner. The marina was an armed camp.

After paying an amount equal to the average monthly wage of a Cuban worker for three bad drinks, we slipped into a modest diner across the street. There, for a couple of bucks each, we enjoyed a delicious dinner of *lechón*, Cuba's national dish of shredded pork, onions, and garlic. Throw in rice and black beans, fried plantains, and yucca, and you have the makings of a feast. After dinner, Bill Williamson, Eric Anderson, and I strolled the narrow, bustling *calles*, or avenues, of old Havana. We soon encountered two stunning young Cuban ladies squeezed into evening dresses that wasted little fabric and left little to the imagination. How old were these girls? we wondered—18? 16? 14? I didn't want to know, but they sure wanted to know us. Soon they were offering their services for less than the price of a drink at La Floridita. We were bailed out of the encounter when Eddie Pilot pulled up and we piled into his car.

Back at Marina Hemingway, we invited Eddie aboard for a nightcap. This was a potentially dangerous proposition for him, since Cubans are strictly forbidden to board visiting boats, but Eddie sat down and had a drink anyway. He seemed to know the marina guards and carried himself with just enough defiance to operate on the edges of Cuba's controlled society. He had been a fighter pilot in Cuba's air force and had completed two tours in Angola. He had also been one of the pilots sent over to retrieve the MiG-21 fighter that another Cuban pilot had flown to Miami in a daring defection a few years before. He loved Miami. He wanted to talk. When Eric told him I was a writer, he became very animated.

He had written a book, still unpublished, about the war and his experiences in Angola. To Cuban men of Eddie's generation—he was probably in his early forties—Angola was their crucible, their Vietnam. Cuba had been the chief supporter of the Communist party during Angola's long civil war. Many young Cubans died on African soil, more than Castro's government has ever admitted, and the war was a terrible drain on the economy and the national spirit. Eddie told us that his book, while not a tell-all exposé, was an accurate account of the war, and that it shed light on the conflict from the perspective of somebody who had fought in it. Although he insisted that it was not remotely anti-Cuban, it was not the kind of book Castro wanted to see published. After another drink, Eddie broached a delicate subject. He wanted to know if I would be willing to smuggle the manuscript out of the country and try to get it published in the United States.

As he left the boat that night, I told him I'd think about it. I told him I had to check with the boat's owner and that I'd let him know the next day. Eddie's predicament, and his risky effort to see his book published, left me feeling small and ungrateful. Lying in my bunk with too many mojitos running around my brain, I thought about the many discussions Carl and I had had about freedom. In a locked-up marina in a locked-down country, freedom had a rarer, much more precious flavor.

Sleep proved elusive. Thinking about Carl left me wondering whether he was in St. Thomas. I thought so. I hoped so. The Hurricane Lenny reports had been confused all day. It was still traveling east. Cuba seemed out of the woods, but the Virgin Islands neighborhood was another story. One report said the storm was weakening, but I knew enough about the unpredictability of tropical storms to know that was not necessarily the last word. What if Carl was still out there? Memories of my own encounters with storms at sea materialized unbidden and chased themselves around my brain.

WHETHER I'm lucky, unlucky, or just plain stupid, I can't judge, but I have sailed through two tropical storms and one hurricane during twenty-five years of conning sailboats across oceans. Each time, the experience was terrifying, humbling, and, in a morbid way, thrilling. Trapped aboard a small boat, I felt perilously close to death and intensely alive.

Tropical Storm Arlene, an unusual early-season storm in 1981, sprang to life, like Lenny, south of Cuba. Arlene went the "right way," westward, toward the Yucatán Straits, which unfortunately was also where I was heading. A week out of Panama, heading home to Miami, I was the inexperienced skipper of a 38-foot sloop, a production boat unprepared for survival conditions. It was early May, and I was not remotely concerned about hurricanes. Not unlike Steve Rigby, I ignored all the classic signs of a brewing cyclone. The boat's engine wasn't working, and it had been a slow passage, made even more so by the calms that preceded the storm. The sails slatted as we drifted on a mirrored sea, 200 miles southeast of the island of Cozumel. I assumed that the long, low, undulating swells rolling in from the east were a sign that the trade winds were on their way. I assured the crew that we'd be sailing again soon, and we began fantasizing about cold beers in Cozumel.

By the time I realized the barometer was freefalling, the sky had darkened and I knew we were in for a blow. Although it was midafternoon, an eerie gray canopy enveloped us as the outer storm bands began to lash the boat. Fortunately, the wind was behind us, and because Arlene had only just formed, the seas had not yet built into the destructive monsters that would wash out much of Cozumel the next day. It is the darkness and the rain that I remember most, a cold, nearly horizontal rain mixed with spume in the fearful gusts. The water stung like swarms of bees. I stood long tricks at the helm, manhandling the wheel through the night. It felt as if the rain was shredding my foul-weather gear. The salt spray stung my eyes. Hunched at the helm, I concentrated on keeping the boat before the wind, hoping for luck or mercy. It was difficult to stay oriented in the absolute darkness, and several times I veered off course, causing the boat to rock violently from side to side. If the seas had been steeper, we would have capsized.

Thankfully, Arlene was in a hurry. By noon the next day the skies had cleared and we were once again becalmed, rolling miserably on leftover swells. When we reached Cozumel a few days later we were shocked at the extent of the damage. With sustained winds of just 50 knots—though with much stronger gusts—Arlene had not even registered on the Saffir-Simpson scale.

Ten years later, when I ran into Hurricane Bob, I was the skipper of a 44-foot sloop, conducting an offshore sailing and navigation passage from St. Thomas, Virgin Islands, to Nassau, Bahamas, with a crew of five inexperienced, middle-aged men. Less than a day from Nassau, we were greeted by a carmine sunrise that poured across the horizon like a malignant cancer. Soon the barometer began to drop, and this time I noticed the plunge right away. A passing freighter informed us that a hurricane had formed just east of us and was moving fast in our direction. We were 50 miles west of San Salvador and about the same distance east of Cat Island. With no time and no place to seek shelter, we could only guard our sea room. I chose to head north-northeast.

It seemed the obvious choice at the time, but in hindsight I know it was wrong. I thought I could dodge the storm and was worried mainly about maintaining sea room. The proper tactic would have been to steer south, close-hauled on starboard tack, heading for the lower left quadrant of the northwest-heading hurricane.

A few hours later the sky darkened and we experienced gale-force winds. Bob seemed like an unwelcome replay of Arlene. It had formed suddenly, close to our position, limiting the fetch required for the seas to become dangerously large, yet the driving rains and shrieking winds that descended upon us as the eyewall approached were terrifying. They tore away my false confidence, although I tried not to reveal my doubts to the crew. While not huge, the seas were steep and washed repeatedly over the boat. I harnessed myself to the helm, shaking like a dog as one wave after another whipped across the deck.

We reached north with just a handkerchief of a headsail propelling us, the mainsail securely lashed to the boom. It was difficult to stand at the helm and nearly impossible to face the wind with eyes open. The counterclockwise circulation was obvious in the ugly storm clouds swirling overhead. As the eye neared, shrill winds made communication impossible. It was hard to think, much less talk. Then something strange happened. Abruptly the winds eased, then went calm, and we found ourselves in the eye of the storm. The entire crew gathered in the cockpit. It was surreal. We were all amazed and encouraged. Having made it through the first half of the hurricane, we vowed to make it through the rest.

The peace lasted less than 20 minutes before we heard the gathering fury of the backside of the cyclone. The winds veered dramatically, from southeast to northwest, and Bob charged toward the northern Bahamas. Later the storm would speed up along the Middle Atlantic coast and slam the Northeast, causing considerable damage from Long Island Sound to the Gulf of Maine. Our strongest sustained winds were in the 70- to 80-knot range, a Category 1 hurricane.

My most recent tropical storm encounter was with Mitch in November 1998. Mitch remains the deadliest Atlantic hurricane on record, leaving more than 18,000 dead and missing in Honduras, Nicaragua, Guatemala, and El Salvador. After cutting a murderous swath along the coast of Central America with winds that reached 160 knots, Mitch fell apart and lumbered into the Yucatán Straits on November 4 as a muddled mass of low pressure. The forecast called for what was left of the once Category 5 storm to head north into the Gulf of Mexico.

I was poised in Ft. Lauderdale, waiting for a decent weather window in which to deliver a new 46-foot sloop to the Virgin Islands. A high-pressure system hovered to the north and looked likely to drop our way, giving us favorable winds and ensuring that the remnants of Mitch would steer clear of our easterly track. I assured my three crew members that this was the perfect moment to shove off. We cleared Port Everglades on November 3 and headed across the Gulf Stream. For two days we enjoyed excellent sailing and managed to claw our way east of the northern Bahamas, but on day three our luck turned.

Instead of dissipating, Mitch regrouped and headed east as a born-again tropical storm. It ripped through the Florida Keys with 60-knot gusts—a frightful encounter for Carl, who was anchored in Key West Harbor when the storm came calling. Mitch then roared north at a forward speed near 40 knots. The weather station at Fowey Rocks off Key Biscayne recorded a 63-knot peak gust on November 5, making Mitch a killer once again. Instead of continuing north, it then turned right, recharged itself in the warm waters of the Gulf Stream, and sprinted through the Bahamas before becoming extratropical.

When I saw the long swells, the falling barometer, and increasing winds from the south, I knew what was coming. We were close-reaching at great speed before a 25-knot southerly when the conditions began to deteriorate rapidly. Soon the winds were gusting to 45 knots, and we were reefed down to storm sails. This time there was plenty of room for the seas to build. Before nightfall we were riding 20-foot combers, mountains of water that packed enormous amounts of destructive energy. I received a position update just before an errant wave silenced my shortwave receiver. Mitch was coming our way, but the eye was forecast to pass about 50 miles north of us. That was close enough. Once again we were on the wrong side of an east-moving storm.

Storms always seem to save their worst mayhem for the dark hours. That night the winds frequently pinned our wind speed indicator to the top of its range, 63 knots. The seas kept building, ultimately to 30 feet. I'd only seen waves like that once before, in the deep reaches of the Southern Ocean during a snorting Cape Horn storm. My crew as Mitch approached consisted of a dear friend, Ed Hershman, who had wanted to make the passage despite a recent car accident that had shattered his leg, and the boat's new owners. The husband was inexperienced but game, but his wife was not. After a nasty fall in the cabin, she retired to her bunk and was rarely seen after that until we made landfall six days later.

Once again the boat was not set up for extreme conditions, and we were forced to rely on the roller-furling genoa for a storm sail. Soon it was reduced to a tiny triangle of Dacron. The mainsail was also controlled with a roller-furling system, very similar to the arrangement on *La Vie en Rose*. I shortened it to about the size of a hand towel. Even with these handkerchief sails, we were making 6 knots while forereaching. The winds peaked around midnight, with gusts that we later learned were over 90 knots. Too exhausted to steer, I eventually managed to get the boat to heave-to. I'll never forget sitting in the cockpit and watching the boat ride up the face of one huge wave after another, only to slide harmlessly to leeward as the waves pressed under the keel. If one had broken over us, it likely would have rolled the boat, but we were lucky.

Mitch timed its assault on the North Atlantic to intercept a fleet of boats taking part in the Caribbean 1500 rally. Fifty-two sailboats, ranging from 30 to 60 feet, had departed Norfolk, Virginia, bound for the British Virgin Islands. Cruising rallies offer a safety-in-numbers approach to passagemaking. Many of the boats and crews were embarking on their first offshore voyage. Rallies can be useful, though they don't appeal to sailors who are loners at heart. Carl Wake sailed the same route a year later, but the thought of participating in a rally probably never crossed his mind.

As the storm track became obvious, many of the boats sought shelter in Bermuda. Some hove-to north of Mitch's intended track, and a few others continued on despite the warnings, hoping to get south ahead of the brunt of the storm. But Mitch was moving too swiftly, and soon they were enduring the same conditions we were. The crew of one boat, a stout 42-foot cutter named *Kampeska*, was fortunate to survive.

According to a detailed two-part account of the incident written by Tom Service in the March and April 1999 issues of

Southwinds magazine, owners Roy and Karen Olson were experienced blue-water sailors. They had logged more than 10,000 offshore miles, and their boat was well suited for passagemaking. Roy's brother and sister-in-law were also aboard. During the night of November 5 the conditions deteriorated to the point where Roy felt he could no longer keep any sail flying. The winds were gusting to 70 knots, according to later Coast Guard reports. Instead of trying to heave-to or running off before the wind, the crew decided to lie ahull—to let the boat drift without any sails set or any pressure on the helm. It was a poor choice, and the boat was battered all night long. Still, they thought the worst was behind them just before dawn on November 6.

Shortly before first light, a sinister wave reared up and struck *Kampeska* on the beam, sending her into a 360-degree roll. When she finally righted herself her hull was intact, but her mast and rigging had been torn away, as had the life raft that had been stored on deck. The mast, still connected by a spiderweb of wire, battered the hull as the boat careened in the huge seas. The crew was battered too. Roy's back was broken, his brother was dazed with a head wound, and the women had suffered broken ribs and various cuts and gashes. They set off an emergency radiobeacon, and 5 hours later a Coast Guard C-130 rescue plane arrived overhead, but it was another full day before the crew of *Kampeska* could be safely airlifted from their disabled vessel.

Mitch roared past us during the night. While the crew of *Kampeska* battled for their lives just north of us, we managed to get underway. The seas were enormous, majestic rollers. From the crests of the waves, the ocean looked like a snow-covered mountain range, more white than blue. We set just enough sail to make speed, gradually unrolling more as conditions improved.

Awake through the night on a boat in a Havana marina, storm images tumbled through my brain in a phantasmagoria. Most sailors never encounter a tropical storm at sea. I must have been unlucky—and, yes, a little bit stupid—to have blundered into three of them. On the other hand, I'd been extraordinarily lucky to have come through all three without losing a boat or even suffering serious injury. What would a Category 4 or 5 storm at sea be like? The prospect was terrifying. Tossing in my bunk, I made a mental checklist of lessons learned.

First, in any storm, the tactic of lying ahull is almost never productive. My experiences have convinced me that a boat is better off when it's moving. It isn't as prone to being knocked down or capsized, and the psychological benefit of forward progress and a proactive approach can't be overstated. I had mentioned this to Carl many times. What to do in heavy weather was one of his favorite topics of conversation.

Second, in a hurricane much stronger than the storms I'd experienced, survival would be unlikely and, in that absolute chaos, would be reduced to a question of luck or grace—not tactics.

Third, when breaking seas surround a boat—seas as high as 50 feet or more, their tops plunging forward in tons of white, oxygenated foam approaching speeds of 40 knots—there is a game of Russian roulette afoot. Just one of those seas scoring a direct hit on a boat can stove its portlights or rip off the deck or the cabintop and will almost certainly roll it over. Then the end may be near. The story of *Kampeska* shows that even in a comparatively weak hurricane, the most seaworthy vessel is just one wave away from disaster.

And finally, the only sure way to survive a hurricane at sea in a small boat is to avoid it. I hoped Carl was avoiding Lenny. Toward dawn, I finally fell asleep, gnawing that bone.

THE LAIR OF THE CYCLOPS

"As anticipated, it proved to be a dirty night. It was exceptionally dark owing to a driving rain, with not a glimpse of moon or stars. The only light was from the phosphorescent tops of the waves, now breaking in every direction, and the fiery wake."

K. Adlard Coles, *Heavy Weather Sailing*

CARL'S relief upon hearing the Monday afternoon report of Lenny's weakening was short-lived. The news early Tuesday morning, November 16, was not so good. Perfect Paul informed him that, instead of continuing to lose strength, the hurricane had reintensified during the night. As of 0800 Atlantic Standard Time, winds were back to 85 knots with higher gusts, making Lenny a dangerous Category 2 hurricane once again. The eyewall was 45 miles wide, and winds of tropical storm force were blowing more than 150 miles from the eye. Barometric pressure is the most accurate measure of a storm's intensity, and Lenny's central pressure, which had risen slightly during the day and early evening hours of November 15, fostering hopes that it might dissipate into a wayward band of rain showers, was falling fast.

This last bit of news could not have surprised Carl, who was no doubt monitoring the old Admiralty barometer mounted on the bulkhead. He was praying that the needle would lean right, toward those hopeful four letters associated with high pressure,

FAIR. Instead the needle was shifting left, past the innocuous CHANGE, beyond dreary RAIN, and toward the all-too-descriptive STORMY near the bottom of the glass. The worst news was that not only was Lenny's wind radius expanding, but the storm had also picked up considerable forward speed during the night. Lenny was heading east at 12 knots.

The center of the storm was located at 15.1° north latitude, 70.5° west longitude, south of Hispaniola. Hurricane-force winds extending 60 to 75 miles ahead of the expanding eye were just 200 miles from Puerto Rico. During the night the National Hurricane Center had upgraded the hurricane watch for Puerto Rico and the Virgin Islands to a hurricane warning, meaning that hurricane conditions were likely within 24 hours. All residents were urged to seek shelter inland immediately.

The forecast called for the storm to begin a gradual turn from east to northeast during the day, making landfall during the night on the southwest Puerto Rican coast, passing directly over the island's rugged interior highlands, then exiting back to sea near San Juan. Even as a Category 2 storm, Lenny promised to be an epic disaster for Puerto Rico. Experts warned that exposed southern harbors were not designed to absorb deadly storm surges. Flash flooding in the mountains would cause already high rivers to overflow their banks. Power outages in the vastly overpopulated greater San Juan area might turn the city into an urban jungle.

Carl plotted Lenny's latest position on the chart. His decision to make all possible speed to the southeast was looking to him like the right one. Despite Lenny's increased speed, it seemed he had a good chance of skirting the storm, though it would be close—too close for comfort. He would experience strong winds, no doubt, but *La Vie* could contend with that.

The question was, could he? He must have wondered for the hundredth time why he had to have the bad luck to encounter a wrong-way hurricane in the middle of November on his first long offshore passage. It didn't seem fair.

The winds were still from the south, although an occasional gust from the southwest allowed him to point *La Vie*'s sleek bow toward the easternmost British Virgin Islands. The winds were freshening, blowing 15 to 20 knots, and *La Vie* was charging along with her sails sheeted tight, throwing sheets of white water from her leeward bow as she plunged through the waves. As mariners used to say, she was carrying a bone in her teeth. She was not a boat that skipped over the seas daintily. She took them head-on, slashing through them with purpose. Low in the water, heavy and deep-keeled, she was wet on deck and uncomfortable in rough conditions, but she was also sure-footed. It would take a violent rogue wave to knock her off her stride. If Carl had had to choose a sailboat in which to be caught in heavy weather, *La Vie* was as good a choice as any.

Carl constantly trimmed his sails to take maximum advantage of the shifting winds, urging every last tenth of a knot from his boat. At some point during the day he must have decided not to attempt a landfall, deeming it too risky. He would wait until he was completely clear of Lenny. At his current speed of 6 to 7 knots he would be approaching the Virgins between midnight and 0400, and he knew that the islands were strewn with rocks, reefs, and wrecks and not well marked for navigating in darkness. Every charter skipper is warned not to sail among the Virgin Islands after dark, and for good reason. Coral-fringed Anegada, just north of the main group of islands, would be the first island Carl encountered. The thought of skirting the fringing reef that drapes around the low, scrub-covered sandspit like a chastity belt in the darkness was terrifying. He'd sailed to Anegada with Tom Criste years before, and he knew how difficult it was to find the entrance through the reef even in broad daylight. There was no way he was going to come close to Anegada at night, especially not with a hurricane breathing down his neck.

By this time Carl was able to pick up Virgin Islands Radio on Channel 401 on his single-sideband radio. With its antenna high in the mountains of St. Thomas, Virgin Islands Radio has a strong signal and can be heard, even on VHF radio, throughout much of the northeast Caribbean. The frequency was buzzing with nervous mariners placing calls and requesting weather updates. The efficient operators remained calm, patiently handling call after call and relaying information. Carl forced himself to eat lunch—quite likely another can of tuna with crackers and a Pepsi—as he listened to the traffic. For several days he had been longing for a decent meal in a restaurant that wasn't bucking up and down, where somebody would serve him food and clean up afterward.

The radio chatter undoubtedly added to his anxiety. He was alone, trying to outflank an unpredictable hurricane, and heading toward a minefield of rocks and small islands. Yet his deep voice, distinctive with its Southern tinge, would have been steady when he responded to the operator's request for a current-conditions update from yachts and commercial vessels throughout the area.

At 1400, when he plotted Lenny's latest coordinates, he noted with relief that although the storm was still tracking at 12 knots, the latitude of its eye was 15.4° north, up from 15.1°. Although that translated into just 18 miles on the water, at least it was an indication that the storm was finally starting to turn. Although the official forecast continued to call for Lenny to head toward Puerto Rico—and although a tropical storm warning and hurricane watch had been issued for the Leeward Islands 3 hours earlier—some of the models were suggesting that a more abrupt turn to the north was in the offing. As long as Lenny turned, Carl could live with the otherwise disquieting news that conditions were favorable for further strengthening.

Sailors are almost always lamenting the wind. There is either too little or too much. Sometime in the morning of November 16, Steve Rigby's whistling, his shaking of the mast, and his pleadings to Buddha finally seemed to pay off with a steady wind. It was from the west, making it a headwind, but that was better than no wind at all. He trimmed in his headsail and mainsail, then eased them out again, then trimmed them once more until they were shaped perfectly. The draft, or belly, of the headsail should be about a third of the way aft when sailing into the wind, while the mainsail's draft should be more toward the middle of the sail. When the telltales on the leading edge of the headsail were streaming aft in perfect unison, Steve focused on keeping them that way with minute adjustments of the tiller. He loved to make a boat sail efficiently. After languishing for nearly a day, *English Braids* was finally making good speed toward the north-northwest. Steve could not quite lay Tortola on that course, but he wasn't overly concerned. It was great to be sailing, to feel the breeze in his face, to be moving at last.

Simon Rigby suspects that his brother wasn't monitoring the single-sideband radio. "The thing probably baffled him," Simon told me, adding that "Steve figured he would have plenty of time to learn how to use it in the upcoming months." He was beyond the range of his VHF radio, a low-wattage device employing very high frequency radio waves that will not bend over the horizon. His maximum VHF range was limited to about 30 or 40 miles when communicating with a powerful shoreside transmitter using a mountaintop antenna, but to no more than 15 or 20 miles—and probably less—if he should try to communicate with another boat. He also had a handheld VHF radio with a range of no more than a few miles. "Steve didn't like to listen to the radio when he was sailing," his wife, Julia, said. "He considered it a distraction." Steve was not worried about the weather. His chief worry was a late arrival in Tortola, which would cause anxiety for Julia.

He knew she'd be worrying about him. He was already overdue. As soon as he was within VHF range he'd call Virgin Islands Radio and patch a call through to her to let her know he was fine. What he didn't know was that Julia was far more than anxious—she was terrified. She'd been monitoring the weather and was well aware that Lenny was bearing down on Puerto Rico and the nearby Virgin Islands. Steve was overdue, and she had to do something. She contacted the Coast Guard and then called the Colgate Offshore Sailing School in Tortola.

"I remember talking to her," says Tyler Pierce of the Offshore Sailing School. "She was really worried. We were frantically canceling classes and tracking down our boats in the BVIs, because it looked like Lenny might score a direct hit. Julia was confused by what the Coast Guard was telling her. I plotted where I thought Steve was and where the hurricane was on a chart and FedExed it up to her in New York."

The west wind built during the day, backing slightly toward the southwest. That slight shift would have lifted Steve more toward his destination were it not that *English Braids* began pounding into the rising seas, which were underlain by an increasingly large western swell. The entire boat would shudder as it fell off the crest of one wave and then was quickly battered by the next. Although the carbon fiber hull was solid, components like the long sprit stored on the foredeck, the twin rudders, and even the canting keel felt loose and vulnerable when the tiny boat was rocked. Steve didn't know yet how much his boat could endure. He probably realized that Alex Bennett had been right—he should have spent some time sailing the boat before shoving off for Tortola. Unlike the heavier *La Vie en Rose*, *English Braids* was designed to skip along the surface of the sea, but there was no skipping in these suddenly rugged conditions. He would have been forced to fall off the wind and ease the sheets a little to give the boat enough power to counter the rising chop.

Perched at the tiller, with his feet propped for support, he steered for hours on end with total concentration. He was an aggressive helmsman by nature, and this was a good time to rely on his instincts. He may even have been enjoying himself despite his increasing weariness, accepting the challenge of trying to con the boat to Tortola. This is what Mini 650 sailors did, and Alex Bennett's stories of interminable hand steering in the Mini Transat after the autopilot failure were fresh in his mind. Perhaps, in part, this was why he had not bothered to repair the autopilot. Julia is convinced that Steve had the skills and mind-set to cope with the worsening conditions and would have relished the challenge of handling the boat in those conditions. He was not one to make excuses. He had told Julia after they purchased *English Braids* that the pressure was on him. "The boat has already proven what she can do. Now it's up to me," he had said.

Steve had spent the previous winter as a sailing instructor in the islands and was no stranger to blustery Caribbean winds. Blustery winds from the west were more rare, though to what extent this registered on him is unknown. At least he was moving more or less in the right direction, and soon he'd be able to call Julia.

Around noon on November 16, Steve was approximately 50 miles east-southeast of St. Croix, the southernmost of the U.S. Virgin Islands, and still 70 miles from the nearest harbor on Tortola. He was tired, and his buttocks and joints ached. He'd been hand steering for nearly 40 hours. He had preprogrammed his handheld GPS before he left Guadeloupe, so he knew the course to steer and the distance to go. He could also read his velocity made good, or VMG—his progress toward his destination—and his estimated time of arrival, or ETA. Although his boat speed was up to 6 knots, his VMG was less than that because he wasn't sailing directly toward his destination. He wouldn't reach Tortola until after midnight unless the wind shifted.

If he could have slipped away from the helm long enough to plot his position on the chart, he might have noticed that he was located over the Saba Bank. In this area of the Caribbean, the ocean floor rises dramatically, from a great depth to as little as 50 feet in a few places. The bank is not usually a hazard to navigation. It is not shallow enough to ground a vessel, so few sailors pay attention to it when they plot their courses across the Caribbean. On this day, however, this flat-topped elevation of the ocean floor was already making the waves steeper and more uncomfortable. The Saba Bank may not be worrisome in normal trade wind conditions, but it is not a place to be in a hurricane.

Sometime in the early afternoon, though he had no way of knowing it, Steve crossed the faded wake left by Guillaume Llobregat's run to the southwest aboard *Frederic-Anne*. Steve was angling up into the Anegada Passage, the wide pass between the Virgin Islands and the northern Leeward Islands where the Caribbean and the Atlantic meet. It's a notoriously rough stretch of ocean. Sailors usually wait for a calm day to cross from the Virgin Islands to St. Martin.

The winds increased in the afternoon, first to a steady 20 knots, then closer to 30, but at least they were backing more to the south. But 30 knots is a lot of wind, nearly gale force, and that force ratchets up in a tiny boat like *English Braids*. Eventually Steve could no longer ignore the fact that he was flying too much sail. First there had been no wind and a few hours later there was too much—he was overcanvased and would have to deal with it. To reduce sail, or reef, in those conditions was not an easy task, especially without an autopilot. First he had to slow down and turn his boat into the wind. The sails flapped madly as he eased the main halyard, the line that raises and lowers the mainsail. Then he hauled in on the reefing outhaul. Fortunately, both of these lines led from the base of the mast back to the cockpit, so Steve was able to reach them while still making periodic lunges to the tiller to keep the boat from bearing off the wind and playing havoc with his task.

The next job was more challenging. He would have had to lash the tiller, let go the headsail halyard, and scurry forward. Working fast, he exchanged the deck-sweeping genoa for a smaller working jib. Reefing is usually done by degrees, so as not to lose too much sail at once, but the winds were really beginning to blow. Quite possibly, as soon as Steve wrestled the sails back up and brought the boat back on course, he realized he still had too much sail up. The only way to get to know a boat is by trial and error. He may well have had to do the maneuver all over again, this time tying a second reef in the mainsail and hoisting his smallest headsail, the storm jib. With that sail configuration he was confident that he could pound his way up to Tortola even if the weather continued to deteriorate.

These were awkward and tiring tasks, even for a fit and agile man. Working aboard an unfamiliar boat that was pitching viciously in unpredictable seas, he probably had to dash back to the cockpit more than once to point the boat back into the wind so that he could complete the sail changes. But his efforts were rewarded. When he once again brought the boat on course, he noticed that the wind had backed still more to the south. Now he was able to steer directly toward Tortola. If he was lucky—and at that moment, despite the ugly winds, he felt lucky—he might just raise the island before midnight.

His next dilemma was whether to attempt a landfall in the dark. He knew the local harbors, including Soper's Hole, Road Town, and the bight of Norman Island, and it would be good to get the boat tied up and collapse into a bunk below. The Salt Island passage from the Caribbean Sea into the relatively protected waters of the Sir Francis Drake Channel is wide enough for night navigation, and he'd been through it many times before. Still, it's not prudent to make landfall in the dark, especially in strong winds on an engineless boat. The memory of his earlier grounding no doubt entered his thoughts.

Carl's decision not to attempt a landfall in the dark was characteristic of him. In the same way, an inclination to make the attempt despite the dangers would have been characteristic of Steve. On the other hand, Steve must have realized by this time that the nasty conditions he was experiencing might be more than just a stalled low-pressure system. He may have decided to postpone a decision until his final approach, while he was still far enough offshore to heave-to safely, and that was hours away.

T HE suddenly rising wind directly over *Frederic-Anne*'s bow slowed her progress on the afternoon of November 16. Guillaume Llobregat and Jacques Santos had likely motored through the night. The winds had been very light, and by lunchtime on November 16 they were well west of the sheer-sided island of Saba. But the weather, and particularly the sea state, had changed abruptly. When the wind backed noticeably toward the south, Llobregat assumed that Hurricane Lenny was making its turn to the north, and the 2 P.M. report from the Hurricane Center seemed to confirm this welcome news. At this point Llobregat made a curious choice.

With *Frederic-Anne* just beginning to labor in the same sloppy seas that were giving the smaller *English Braids* fits, Llobregat decided to turn his schooner around and head back toward St. Martin. *Frederic-Anne* was approximately 90 miles west-southwest of her home island and 25 miles southeast of St. Croix. Llobregat seems to have concluded that with Lenny altering its track to the northeast, *Frederic-Anne* would be able to stay south of the worst of the storm and still be in a position to return to Marigot by late the next day, November 17, or early on the day after that.

Another sailor might have fled south to evade Lenny and stayed there until the hurricane was safely past, and indeed that had been Llobregat's original plan. But instead he had run west-southwest and was now turning back at the first hint of the hurricane turning north. His actions were like those of a man sidestepping a hulking brute on a city side-walk—giving way, but only grudgingly, altering his path the bare minimum to avoid a head-on encounter. He had been forced by Bobby's Marina to ride out the hurricane at sea, and now he would suffer no more delay to his charter season than absolutely necessary. Most likely this had been his plan since the day before: Brush against the bottom of the storm out to the west of St. Martin, and ride the westerly storm winds back home. *Frederic-Anne* would be taking the seas from astern, making the ride more tolerable and at the same time keeping breaking seas away from her vulnerable deckhouse windows and foredeck hatches. If this was his plan, it was an audacious one, one that only a supremely confident sailor—a sailor, for example, who had already demonstrated his ability to singlehand his big schooner on a long ocean passage—would contemplate.

Once having made this decision, Llobregat tried to patch a call to Alicia and his family through Radio France in Martinique. He couldn't get through, however, and he never was able to make radio contact with home. Although the winds continued to increase, Llobregat assured Santos that things wouldn't get any worse and that they would be back home soon.

With the winds gusting above 20 and then 30 knots as the afternoon wore on, Llobregat and Santos reduced sail by stages, first dropping the huge mainsail and then the flying, or forward-most, jib. These measures took pressure off the bowsprit and eased the tendency of the wheel and rudder to drive the boat into the wind. Next they tied a reef in the gaff-rigged foresail, which was smaller and farther forward than the mainsail. The gaff, a spar across the head of the four-cornered sail, helped steady it in strong winds but flogged about like a medieval war club until the halyard was tensioned. The reefed foresail and small staysail left the schooner with a simple, balanced sail plan to cope with the rising winds. That done, Llobregat and Santos jogged slowly eastward, awaiting the next hurricane update.

Studying the chart, Llobregat probably noticed that his east-bound track, which was offset slightly south of the track he'd followed west, would take *Frederic-Anne* close to the Saba Bank. This would have concerned him, but his options were limited. With near gale-force winds still backing into the south, he was committed to passing north of Saba Island, because passing south would have risked making Saba—perhaps even St. Eustatius and St. Kitts—into dangerous lee shores. By steering north of Saba, Llobregat could keep more sea room under his port bow, but he was also steering his boat closer to Lenny's path.

Despite the vastness of the sea, it doesn't take much to make a sailor feel trapped.

On the afternoon of November 16, Hurricane Hunter aircraft confirmed that Lenny was strengthening rapidly. The storm had grown to sustained winds between 85 and 100 knots in the wall of its large eye, and hurricane-force winds extended well beyond the center, especially to the east and southeast. As of 5 P.M., or 1700 hours Atlantic Standard Time, Lenny's eye was near 15.8° north latitude and 68.2° west longitude.

Lenny was moving northeast at 14 knots, its track over the past 12 hours making a shallow arc north rather than the expected abrupt turn. The National Hurricane Center's 5 P.M. intermediate advisory finally conceded that Lenny was likely to continue its present course for the next 24 hours at least. A hurricane warning was issued for St. Martin, St. Barts,

Anguilla, Saba, St. Eustatius, and St. Kitts, while the hurricane watch for the western portion of the Dominican Republic was discontinued. It now seemed likely that Puerto Rico and the central cluster of the Virgin Islands, lying north of the track, would be on Lenny's less dangerous side and would be spared the worst. But the island of St. Croix, 35 miles south of the other U.S. Virgins, lay directly in Lenny's path and little more than 200 miles away. The storm was expected to make landfall on St. Croix in 14 or 15 hours.

Huge swells were already crashing on the western shores of Saba, St. Martin, St. Barts, and Anguilla. The effects of the hurricane were being felt as far away as Colombia, where a fishing boat had been overturned by huge swells. In Tobago, hundreds of miles to the south, the BBC reported that 12-foot waves were washing up on unprotected western beaches.

Nothing was certain, of course. The average error in the predicted track of a Caribbean hurricane is 100 miles for each 24 hours into the future, and the National Hurricane Center's forecast errors for Lenny would later be shown to have ranged from 5 to 33 percent higher than average.

Just where was this one-eyed monster headed? The only thing anybody knew for sure was that it wasn't turning hard left, and that translated into mounting terror for three sailboats and their grim-faced crews.

CARL WAKE felt trapped as *La Vie en Rose* plunged into rapidly building seas. Like Steve Rigby, he was probably stunned at how quickly the winds and seas had built. Carl was thankful for the roller-furling systems that allowed him to reef his sails from the sanctuary of the cockpit. He wanted no part of *La Vie*'s narrow, pitching foredeck. All afternoon he had systematically shortened sail, taking in a little on the jib and then a bit of the mainsail. The process was simple: Ease out a bit of jibsheet, then crank in the jib furling line. Ease out a bit of the main outhaul, then take in the main furling line. Carl was able to tend these lines while the autopilot steered, a stark contrast to the brute physical labor of shortening sail on the pitching decks of *English Braids* and *Frederic-Anne*.

La Vie had made terrific progress and was in the Anegada Passage well before dark. The winds, however, continued to back into the south while building, so that Carl eventually found himself headed toward Anguilla and St. Martin and was forced to tack over to a southwesterly heading. He clearly felt that his best and perhaps only option was to continue in a generally southerly direction, hoping to leave Lenny to starboard as the storm continued its east-northeast course.

The Caribbean islands, those gleaming jewels of sand and palms that Carl had been pushing toward and dreaming about through eleven days at sea, were now his major concern. Islands and storms don't mix. Rock and fiberglass don't mix. Sailors are taught that if they're caught in severe conditions, they should remain at sea. It's foolhardy to make a mad dash for a safe harbor. Instead, maintain sea room. Steer for the open ocean, where there's room to run away from or at least ride out the storm without the threat of being dashed to bits on something hard. This timeworn philosophy has been drilled into sailors from Odysseus on down. Like so much sea wisdom developed before the advent of GPS, accurate weather forecasts, vastly improved communications systems, efficient sail-handling equipment, and reliable diesel engines, however, the belief in maintaining sea room at all costs is not as accepted as it once was.

Today, most sailors try to reach shelter when a storm threatens. They'd rather take their chances tied to a dock, not pitching about in a storm-tossed sea. They say they'd rather lose their boats than their lives, and it's hard to argue with that. Also, while modern boats are marvels of design and engineering, their voluminous hull shapes are often not as seakindly, especially in severe conditions, as their wooden or even early fiberglass predecessors. Many of today's boats are incapable of heaving-to, a technique that allows a boat to lie against the wind comfortably in storm conditions. And sailors themselves have changed. Today's cruisers are not the grizzled mariners of old. They're often middle-aged or retired couples engaged in a one- or two-year sabbatical cruise and without a lot of offshore sailing experience. They are devotees of information and spend considerable time obtaining and analyzing weather data. Their plan is not to prepare themselves or their boat to ride out a storm with plenty of sea room, but to gather enough data to avoid severe weather altogether. Unfortunately, sailing doesn't always go according to plan.

Carl had steered *La Vie en Rose* into a serious predicament. As he forged south, deeper into the Anegada Passage, his sea room became limited. Anegada Island and the rest of the British Virgins lay to starboard. St. Martin, Anguilla, and St. Barts lay to port. Although the two island groups were nearly 100 miles apart, 100 miles is hardly a long way when a hurricane is in hot pursuit. Sailing south would also take him closer to Lenny—unless, as Carl must still have assumed, the hurricane was poised to make its long-forecast turn north. Saba and St. Croix also lay south, but those more distant obstacles would have to wait their turn. One thing at a time, and in the meantime, the nearby presence of the islands he had sailed toward for eleven days and dreamed of for years had to have been strangely reassuring for a first-time passagemaker so long at sea. Perhaps Carl still did not feel his situation was desperate. Perhaps he was still confident that he'd skirt the storm. But his tactic, really, wasn't all that different from an automobile driver trying to beat a train to a railroad crossing—with the added wrinkle that the side of the hurricane Carl was dashing toward was precisely the wrong side to be on.

Although Carl's tactics were driven to some extent by Lenny's unpredictable track, if he had truly believed in the "sea room is safe" approach he could have stayed clear of the Anegada Passage altogether. He could have kept sailing east, out into the broad Atlantic. Instead, he was drawn toward the islands like a lemming to a cliff.

THE EDGE OF
CONTROL

"The sea—this truth must be confessed—has no generosity."

Joseph Conrad, *The Mirror of the Sea*

B<small>Y</small> late afternoon on November 16, *English Braids* was getting tossed about in the Anegada Passage like a sock in a washing machine. Steve Rigby had done a remarkable job of pushing north through rapidly deteriorating conditions. Around this time there was an unconfirmed report from a ham radio operator on the east end of Tortola of a 110-knot gust. It is safe to say that the winds in Lenny's outermost bands were gusting to well over 60 knots from east of south. The sky was a sickening gray as twilight approached, the gathering clouds swirling counterclockwise with increasing speed. The wind was starting to shriek. The waves were being blown apart as they crested, whipping white foam into the air. Rigby had most likely dropped his storm jib, lashed it to the foredeck, and was pushing on under deeply reefed mainsail alone.

"The Mini would have been terribly uncomfortable in those conditions," says Alex Bennett. "We experienced similar conditions at the start of leg one in the 1999 Transat. It was wild. The boat was all over the place. Steve probably had decent control up to a point. But once he encountered hurricane-force winds—well, that's another thing altogether. Minis are very hard to keep control of." Only hours before, Steve had been bobbing on a calm sea. Now he was in a fight with a heavyweight.

Steve's wife, Julia, wanted to know how he was faring. She implored the Coast Guard to contact him, and U.S. Coast Guard Greater Antilles Section (GANTSEC) in San Juan, Puerto Rico, responded by putting out an urgent Pan-Pan alert on VHF Channels 16 and 22-A and on the single-sideband emergency frequency, 2182 kHz, asking all vessels to be on the lookout for a 21-foot sailboat named *English Braids*. The boat was overdue in Tortola and might be in distress.

Just after 7 P.M., or 1900 hours AST, the cruise ship *Nordic Express* informed the Coast Guard that it had made radio contact with Steve. After telling him that a dangerous hurricane was on a course to overrun *English Braids*, the cruise ship radio officer asked Rigby if he wanted to be picked up. Steve replied that he would continue to sail. He was 32 miles southeast of Tortola and had the wind behind him. He was flying, and if he could hold the boat together he was just 3 or 4 hours from landfall. He must have believed he could beat Lenny into port. There was simply no way he was going to abandon his boat and his dream.

But Steve Rigby did not yet know the limits of his boat—the edge of the zone of safety beyond which *English Braids* would become unstable, uncontrollable, or both. Nor could he yet appreciate how sharp that edge was for his boat. On a boat like *La Vie en Rose* or the boats on which Steve had taught New Yorkers to sail, there are warning signs—a gradual loss of steering, a queasy sense that the boat is responding atypically—but nothing is gradual on a high-strung rocket ship like *English*

Braids, with its canting keel, its tandem rudders, its saucer hull. On a boat like that, you can be over the edge before you realize you've reached it.

Shortly after his contact with the *Nordic Express*, something may have gone wrong for Rigby. Exactly what and when is unclear, but within an hour—perhaps just a few minutes—he was back on the radio, this time with rising urgency in his voice. And this time he was transmitting on his handheld VHF radio, which had a maximum range of just a few miles. Something had happened to his installed VHF with its masthead antenna and much longer range. The most likely explanation is that Rigby had lost either the antenna or possibly the mast itself.

The sun had set somewhere behind the thick clouds of the gathering storm at 5:47 P.M., and by the time Rigby spoke with *Nordic Express*, the darkness was total, making it more difficult for him to anticipate and avoid breaking seas. He had been sailing downwind on the edge of control for at least 3 hours, and he had been hand steering without a break for more than two days. Even a moment's inattention could have caused an uncontrolled jibe—with the wind unexpectedly filling the sail from the opposite side and sending the boom crashing across the boat—quite possibly buckling the mast. Maybe his headsail was not lashed well enough on the foredeck, and a wave swept the deck and washed it overboard, still attached to the boat. He would have had to let go of the tiller, dash forward, and try to haul it back aboard. The boat might have jibed while he was corralling the sail.

Alternatively, perhaps *English Braids* was knocked down by a powerful wave to the point of submerging her mast in the sea. A knockdown is not quite as destructive as a full capsize, but it can easily take the mast out of a boat. The seas, though still traveling primarily southwest to northeast, were confused, and a confused sea is the most dangerous condition for a small boat.

But the confusion was not limited to the seas. Julia Rigby, waiting anxiously by her phone in New York, would soon be caught in the middle of a tug of war between the Coast Guard and her husband. Julia doesn't think that *English Braids* had been disabled or that Rigby had given up on bringing his boat through the storm. "I am convinced that Steve was doing okay, that he was still sailing," Julia explained later, "but the Coast Guard was convinced otherwise. They seemed to think that just because his boat didn't have an engine he was disabled. I had to convince them that it didn't have an engine because it was a race boat, a sailboat. They didn't understand. They were insistent that he leave the boat."

Assuming *English Braids* had been knocked down, which is not uncommon for a small boat in severe weather, Steve would have had to react very fast. Not only must you hold onto the boat to prevent being washed overboard in a knockdown, but you must take the pressure off the sails. Steve would have clutched the high side of the boat with one arm and frantically tried to reach and release the mainsheet with the other. Suddenly he would have been standing upright, parallel with the deck, looking straight down into the maw of the Caribbean. That's a window on the world that a sailor never forgets and hopes never to see again.

Knockdowns usually result in damage to the lee side of a boat, the side that is driven into the seas—not the windward side, where the wave actually strikes. In extreme cases the hull can be stove in. In a severe gale off Bermuda many years ago, my 32-foot sloop sustained damage to its rigging, sails, stanchions, and lifelines when it was knocked flat. I had the same momentary view that Steve might have had before I was carried off the boat by a cascade of water. Miraculously—I never knew how—I was able to pull myself back aboard after the boat righted itself. Although it was floating, the boat was a disaster. In a few seconds our orderly world had become chaos. We were hit with such force that the dividers—a compasslike instrument used for measuring distances on a chart—flew through the air and buried its twin points in the fiberglass cabintop. The conditions at the time were similar to what Steve was contending with in the Anegada Passage. In the black, wind-whipped Caribbean Sea, Steve Rigby knew he was in serious trouble but also, apparently, believed that he might still save his boat.

If *English Braids* went over, she must have righted herself with Rigby still aboard. He was a strong man with huge hands and would have held on for all he was worth. If that was how he lost his VHF antenna, the mainsail was very likely shredded and the rig damaged. He would have had to summon what was left of his strength for another trip forward. Securing his safety harness to the boat, he would have pulled himself inch by inch toward the mast. If the mast was still standing, he would have had to wrestle down what was left of the mainsail. If it wasn't, he would have had to cut away the spar and rigging as quickly as possible with bolt cutters or a hacksaw before the broken mast became a deadly battering ram and poked a hole in the hull.

"In conditions like those, Steve had no choice but to get all sail down," says Alex Bennett. "The Mini is pretty buoyant, but at some point, she's going to be knocked over. I am not sure what I would have done, but in the ultimate survival conditions I think I would have tried to cut the mast away. Then the boat would be one big, miserable life raft, but at least you'd have a chance."

That may well have been a decision made for Steve by the sea, but Julia doesn't think so. "The messages relayed to me by the Coast Guard and Virgin Islands Search and Rescue from Steve did not imply that he had lost the mast, or that he was in immediate danger," she says.

Groping along the deck, Rigby must have battled his emotions as well as the rising wind and seas. This was not part of the script, or maybe it was. Maybe Buddha was testing him. If he survived this ordeal, he'd have forged a bond with *English Braids* that would be unbreakable. If they survived Lenny together, the 2001 Mini Transat would seem like a casual cruise in New York Harbor. Whether the mast was still up or not, without any sail he had very limited steerage and no way to influence the boat's motion or direction. Lashing the tiller, Steve made his way below to try to monitor the VHF radio.

In the tiny, spare cabin, Steve must have braced himself as best he could while the seas roared in from the southwest and the boat lurched hard to starboard, again and again. The cabin was a disaster. Gear was flung about everywhere, and several inches of water sloshed about, soaking everything. Perhaps he heard the frantic chatter on the bulkhead-mounted VHF radio and gave thanks that it still worked. He grabbed the mike and tried to call Virgin Islands Search and Rescue, but there was no response.

He was still able to receive without a functioning antenna, but he was no longer able to transmit, at least not very far, and his calls went unheard, swallowed by the howling storm. Realizing what was wrong, he must have found his handheld radio in the chaos of the cabin and tried to reach Virgin Islands Search and Rescue on that, but handheld radios have a maximum range of just a few miles.

He could not reach the Virgin Islands, but a nearby sailor heard him loud and clear. Steve Rigby heard a deep, soft voice with a kindly Southern accent.

"*English Braids*, this is *La Vie en Rose*. Do you copy?"

THE HEART
OF THE STORM

"There is an ecstasy that marks the summit of life, and
beyond which life cannot rise. And such is the paradox of
living, this ecstasy comes when one is most alive, and it
comes as a complete forgetfulness that one is alive."

Jack London, *The Call of the Wild*

VIRGIN ISLANDS Search and Rescue (VISAR) was
established in 1988 out of concern for the safety of bareboat
charterers—sailors who opted to rent yachts without a professional captain or crew. "We realized that if we had a problem
with one of the bareboats, we had no real plan in place to
launch a proper rescue," explains Barney Crook, owner of
Tortola Marine Management in Road Town, Tortola. TMM,
one of the most respected bareboat charter operations in the
Caribbean, donated office space to VISAR in the early days.
"We had an informal search-and-rescue group, like a makeshift
volunteer fire department, but there was the potential for a real
disaster that might be devastating to the industry. We knew we
needed something more organized. Although we started with
just a handful of volunteers and one old lifeboat, we had big
plans and modeled VISAR on the Royal National Lifeboat
Institution. By the time Lenny came calling, we had two 22-
foot rigid inflatables and a pretty effective communications

network." The RIBs would be of little use in Lenny, but the communications network would prove its value.

Although Carl Wake and Steve Rigby had begun their respective passages days removed and thousands of miles apart, their boats were very close when Wake heard Rigby's increasingly urgent VHF calls. Carl called Steve directly, and Steve responded, informing Carl that he didn't know if his radio was transmitting properly. Carl told Steve that his signal was feeble, then patched Rigby's message through to VISAR. With Carl acting as intermediary, the VISAR operator let Steve know that Julia was in contact with the Coast Guard. Lenny was intensifying, VISAR reported, and things were going to get worse before they got better. Though his boat was battered, Steve was greatly relieved to be in radio contact. Through Carl, he urged VISAR to call Julia directly and let her know he was okay.

The Hurricane Center's 8 P.M. AST update would shortly report that Lenny's sustained winds were up to 100 knots, making it a Category 3 hurricane. Six years later, Katrina would be a Category 3 storm when it demolished New Orleans and swamped the Gulf Coast. Lenny's central barometric pressure was 959 millibars and continuing to fall. Its center was at 15.9° north latitude and 67.6° west longitude—30 miles north of its position 6 hours earlier, but almost 90 miles east. This was not the turn forecasters had expected. The large, sprawling system was revolving about a point 140 miles south of the Mona Passage, which separates the island of Hispaniola from Puerto Rico.

Satellite photos and continuous loops of the storm confirm that its outermost bands, which were by this time pummeling the south coast of Puerto Rico, were also lashing Carl and Steve in the Anegada Passage with sustained winds from the south-

southeast near 50 knots, gusting to 70. The rain was heavy, the seas at least 20 feet and building. A 1-knot current running counter to a wave can double its height, and those places in the world's oceans where powerful currents routinely clash with prevailing seas—such as the Agulhas Current off South Africa —are notoriously deadly. The current in the Anegada Passage was setting southwesterly—as it often does in November— right into the teeth of the seas that had been building for days from the southwest and south before the wind had swung into the southeast. Though the speed of the current was only about half a knot, it was enough to increase wave heights by as much as 50 percent, at the same time making the waves both steeper and more liable to break.

Relaying its messages through VISAR and Carl, the Coast Guard, aware of Rigby's peril, urged him to abandon his boat and attempt to get aboard the larger, more seaworthy *La Vie en Rose*. This was an extreme recommendation. Sailboat-to-sailboat rescues in near-hurricane conditions are almost unheard of. Julia couldn't understand why, if the situation was so critical, the Coast Guard didn't pick up Steve itself.

The Coast Guard could have offered several good reasons. With their cutters diverted to the south, a helicopter rescue would have been their only option, but their nearest helicopters, HH-65 Dolphins, were at Air Station Borinquén in Aguadilla, on the northwest tip of Puerto Rico. Aguadilla was 190 miles away, and the Dolphins have a 350-mile operational range. Had a chopper been sent to rescue Steve, it could not have been overhead for 2 hours—longer if it stopped to refuel en route at St. Thomas or Beef Island in the BVIs—and then it would have had to find him. If it didn't refuel while outbound, it would have lacked enough fuel to return to base and would have had to land somewhere else instead. St. Croix was the most likely option, but landing there in the midst of the storm would not have been easy. Assuming the helicopter crew could find Steve, the rescue itself would have been conducted in darkness—increasing the difficulty and danger severalfold—and a rescue from the deck of Steve's bucking boat would have been impossible. He would have had to jump in the water before the rescue could be attempted. Nothing obligates the Coast Guard to place their personnel in extreme danger when a risk-reward calculation advises against it. And in this case there was another boat—an "asset," in Coast Guard terminology—standing by on scene and willing to help.

But the reason the Coast Guard gave Julia was the last possible one, which was that Steve had not issued a Mayday. For reasons of pride, guilt, optimism, a stubborn refusal to accept what was happening, or all of these together, Steve could not bring himself to do that. And there was another factor inclining Steve to cling to his boat as if to flypaper. According to Julia, he did not know how to swim. For a man who sought out physical challenges and was making the sea his life, this was an extraordinary shortcoming, and now it loomed large. Steve knew that a Coast Guard rescue would require him to jump into the ocean. He would be wearing a life jacket, but the prospect of a first swim at night in a storm, miles from the nearest land, had to have been terrifying.

Carl relayed the Coast Guard's message to Steve and added that he was standing by. *English Braids* was rolling gunwale to gunwale, and breaking waves were sweeping the deck. Steve knew that his boat might not bob back upright if the wrong wave caught her at the wrong moment. With no sail set, he was for the most part drifting. If his tiny boat did hold together and remain afloat, there was a good possibility that she'd be dashed against the rocky shores of one of the several islands spread out like a minefield over the horizon to leeward. It was time for a decision.

"He did not want to abandon the boat," Julia insists. "He made that clear." The Coast Guard, however, asked Julia to urge Steve to do just that, and finally, reluctantly, she agreed. "You have to trust the Coast Guard," she explains. "Steve had told me to call the Coast Guard if anything went wrong. He trusted the Coast Guard. If the Coast Guard is telling you your husband should abandon his boat, what do you do?" When the Coast Guard passed along Julia's message via VISAR and *La Vie en Rose*, Steve knew what he had to do.

Carl had continued to shorten sail as the wind intensified, rolling his mainsail into the mast and his jib on its furler. The remaining scrap of mainsail looked like a pennant flying rigidly from the mast, and the jib was reduced to the size of a beach towel. These tiny sails were enough to propel *La Vie en Rose* forward while allowing the autopilot to steer the boat. Dressed down to storm canvas, *La Vie* was coping with the wild conditions.

After pulling on his heavy foul-weather gear to combat the stinging rain that accompanied each powerful gust, Carl was coping too. He was apparently still convinced that if he could just continue to push south, he'd outflank Lenny eventually and sail clear of the madness. Like many a sailor in severe weather, he felt the sort of kinship with his boat that only dependency breeds. A sailor in a storm talks to his boat, stroking her fiberglass decks and willing her through the blow. She is far from an inanimate object then; she is a partner and protector with an intertwined fate.

But now Carl faced an obligation that trumped even his urgent imperative to forge south. He had become, by virtue of a geographic twist, the point man in what would be a dangerous and potentially disastrous rescue at sea. He knew that every minute he delayed would leave him more vulnerable to Lenny's approach. An accident of fate had thrust him into a position for which he was unprepared by experience and temperament.

He was thankful that the cantankerous autopilot had worked so far, but he was unsure whether or how to stop the boat. If he slowed down too much, he'd become a bobbing duck for the next breaking wave. He dreaded making a hash of it and leaving *La Vie* broadside to the seas. Experimenting, he may have rolled in what was left of the headsail and eased the mainsheet to allow the mainsail to luff from time to time. This slowed the boat to a knot or two, but the motion was awkward, and Carl knew that *La Vie* would be vulnerable without her jib.

"*La Vie en Rose, La Vie en Rose,* this is *English Braids.*" Steve's voice was soft and distant, but his accent, a pleasing combination of English and Australian, was unmistakable. Carl dashed below to the VHF radio mounted above the nav station and quickly replied, "This is *La Vie en Rose.*"

"*La Vie en Rose,* are you prepared to take me off my boat?"

"I am, and I am standing by. What is your exact position?"

Steve gave Carl the coordinates from his GPS receiver, and Carl entered them as a waypoint in his own GPS, which then gave him the direction and distance to *English Braids.* Amazingly, she was just a few miles away.

"Do you have any lights showing?" Carl would have asked Steve. In the night and the dense gloom of the hurricane's outer bands, with rain driving almost horizontally, visibility was practically nonexistent. It is quite likely that *English Braids* had no working lights at this point, having been swept repeatedly by breaking seas. Carl told Steve that he would steer an intersecting course, instructing him to stand by with a flare.

Carl had to have wondered how he, a neophyte, had become the would-be rescuer of a fellow sailor in a hurricane. He had no experience in high-seas rescues, nor in his compulsive consumption of nautical stories had he read or heard of any sailor accomplishing such a rescue in a hurricane. A sailboat, especially one with a small, inefficient engine, was about the worst possible platform for what he was going to attempt—to rescue a man from another sailboat that was essentially adrift.

Alex Bennett, who has himself been rescued from two sinking yachts, believes that the only conceivable rescue scenario required Carl to maneuver close enough to windward of Steve's foundering boat to get a line and a float to him, but not too close. If the boats collided, *La Vie* might be holed, and it would be easy to tangle rigs as the boats rolled viciously back and forth in the huge waves. If *La Vie* lost her mast she'd be as helpless as *English Braids*.

Carl could just sail away, and no one would ever know. He could say he hadn't been able to find Steve, or that he was in danger himself and had to bear away; no one would ever blame him. That would have been the prudent thing to do. His own life and boat were in jeopardy, and he was no master mariner. He was an old army man masquerading as a sailor. The task he faced was better left to professionals.

But I'm certain that Carl never seriously considered that way out. He knew what he had to do, even if he wasn't sure how to do it. It was all about duty versus freedom for Carl Wake; decisions always came down to that. I can hear him sighing, saying yet again that you are never really free to make your own choices, but you are free to decide to do your duty. He had to help Steve Rigby. This was what he had gone to sea for, to test himself, to find out who he was, what he was capable of.

He already knew what he wasn't capable of; his life had shown him that all too clearly. This time he wouldn't fall short, not now, not here. He would save Steve Rigby or die trying. I can hear him mustering his resolve, saying, "Here we go, Wake, pull yourself together. Time to get after it."

"I don't know how they managed to pull off the transfer," Alex Bennett says, "but I can tell you, from practical experience, rescues at sea are iffy and require skill and luck. In those conditions, it would require a lot of luck." Bennett describes being picked up by the Coast Guard when the large racing trimaran *King Philip* sank out from under its crew in the North Atlantic. "There's a moment when you are not sure you're going to survive. You have to remain very clearheaded when you're in the water.

"There is no way the two boats could have come alongside or even close to each other," Bennett continues. "I'm impressed that they even managed to find each other in those conditions. It is so easy to sail right past another boat, even one very close at hand, and not see it. Steve must have tied a line to himself and been pulled through the water by Carl, and Carl must have done a great job of controlling his boat. Getting Steve aboard would not have been easy. It was extraordinary seamanship, but they needed luck, too."

As *La Vie en Rose* sailed toward *English Braids*, both sailors longed for just a trace of visibility, but there was none. If they'd initiated the rescue a few hours earlier they would have had a fading light to work with, but now the gloom was profound. Carl had probably unrolled a tiny bit of jib again to help the autopilot steer. He peered intently over the spray dodger, searching for *English Braids*, scanning the sea ahead with binoculars. Maybe the two men remained in contact by VHF, and when Carl's GPS showed them close, Steve fired a flare. Or maybe Carl simply homed on the GPS waypoint until he started getting intermittent glimpses of the tiny sloop nearby through the blinding rain and mountainous seas. Perhaps he tried to train his binoculars, but the pitching of *La Vie* and the horrible rolling of *English Braids* made it difficult to focus. One moment the stricken boat looked fine, but a moment later she would be laid on her beam ends when a wave broke over her, and a moment after that she would disappear altogether behind a rearing sea.

Carl used his handheld VHF to tell Steve he had him in sight, and Rigby climbed into the cockpit. Seeing *La Vie en Rose* close by must have been an incredible relief. He had lashed a waterproof bag with an EPIRB, his passport, boat papers, money, and a few other documents in his small backpack and tied it around his waist. He couldn't put it on his back, because he already had a life jacket—a "personal flotation device" in Coast Guard parlance—lashed in place. He knew he was going to need all his considerable strength for the upcoming maneuver. I can picture Carl waving, then disengaging the autopilot and taking manual control of the helm. He steered as close as he dared, but his initial approach—if characteristically cautious—would have placed him too far to windward, as much as several hundred yards away. Always a gentleman, he may have shouted a greeting and an introduction to Steve, but the wind tore the words from his mouth and carried them away. Steve's response, if he made one, was blown back in his face. Even if the men were talking by handheld VHF, communication was virtually impossible. Before

Carl could work out how to close the gap or rig enough line to span it, *La Vie* may have sailed past. That meant he would have to tack, and somehow he was going to have to stop.

Carl knew that tacking in those seas was a risky proposition, especially with his handkerchief sails. If he stalled after turning into the wind, he would be at the mercy of any wave that chose that moment to break over him. He would have to time his tack with the waves, turning hard as he skidded down a wave face into the trough so as to force the bow through the wind and fill the sails on the other tack before the next sea reached him. Realizing he'd have better control with the engine running, he pressed the starter button and held his breath. The Volvo diesel had never started smoothly, but after a few reluctant growls it rumbled to life. Carl knew this would also be a good time to charge his batteries for the long night ahead.

Carl may have sailed well past Steve Rigby, perhaps losing *English Braids* astern in the darkness and rain, the mountainous seas and spindrift, as he looked for the perfect moment to tack. Finally he knew he had to go for it, and while riding down the face of a wave, he spun the wheel to port. Suddenly he was in the trough, a canyon of water with almost no wind. He let go the starboard-side jibsheet and frantically pulled in the one to port, but *La Vie* was stalling. His heart hammering in his chest, he quickly pushed the throttle forward. The prop dug in and *La Vie* continued around. Then she rose to the next wave and began to regain her stride. Carl finished sheeting in the sail, thankful the maneuver was complete. Merely tacking in a storm of this magnitude was an accomplishment. He wanted a cigarette.

La Vie en Rose quickly closed the distance back to *English Braids*. After sailing hard on the wind for two days, Carl found the conditions less intimidating with the wind aft of the beam.

This time he may have sailed closer, passing downwind of *English Braids*. As he neared Steve, he let the jib luff to slow down, and it flailed violently. He may have shouted across the water or into the radio that he would tack again, sail upwind of Steve, and heave-to. Then he'd float a line back to him. Steve would have to jump in the water and grab the line. "Pull it twice when you have it and I will pull you in. We'll have to work fast."

Once again Carl had to tack his boat in a raging storm. This time he knew that the engine was a vital part of the equation. Timing it carefully, he put *La Vie* through the wind and gathered way on starboard tack. As he reeled *English Braids* back into sight, he thought through his next maneuver. Heaving-to is much like tacking, except that the leeward jibsheet is not released. Instead the jib is allowed to back, or fill with wind on the wrong side of the sail. In this position it tries to force the bow away from the wind, an effort that is counterbalanced by the mainsail and rudder. Suspended in a tenuous equilibrium, a properly hove-to boat lies roughly 50 to 60 degrees off the wind and drifts slowly to leeward. Waves rarely break over a hove-to boat because the natural slick caused by the drifting hull has a calming effect on approaching seas. Heaving-to is effective in gales, or even in storm conditions before seas become dangerously large. In a hurricane, however, slick or no slick, sooner or later a wave will flatten any boat.

I think it likely that Carl made his next approach perhaps 200 yards to windward of *English Braids*, then turned into the wind. He did not release the jibsheet. *La Vie* shuddered, but eventually the sail backed and the boat came to rest. The momentary strain on the rig was frightening, but it held together. Carl was relieved, even a little heady. He had heaved-to in conditions that would have intimidated any mariner. "You keep learning new tricks," he thought.

Quite possibly, however, he was still too far away from Steve and would have to do it again. It may have taken a few more tries before he was satisfied that *La Vie* was in the right position, for it was nearly impossible to gauge how far and fast *La Vie* was going to drift. When he was about 100 yards directly upwind of *English Braids*, he was at last satisfied, but now there was no time to lose. He would have to find his longest line—if it wasn't already at hand—tie a float to it, and pay it back to Steve, all while staying prepared to peel away if he seemed about to drift down on top of the smaller boat. He was suddenly very tired.

His longest lines, his anchor rodes, were forward in the anchor locker, but he can't have had time to make his way to the bow and drag an anchor line back to the cockpit, and the trip over the deck would have been difficult and dangerous in those conditions. Instead he must at some point have dug out the several spare lines he kept in his cockpit locker, each nearly 100 feet long, and lashed them together. He could never remember how to tie a double sheet bend, and instead made interlocking loops with bowlines. He trusted his bowlines and always suspected his other knots. Needing a float, he considered the horseshoe buoy mounted on *La Vie*'s stern but thought better of it. He might need to deploy that when Steve got closer to the boat. He then grabbed a PFD and lashed it to the end of the line along with the rescue strobe light from the horseshoe. By the time he assembled his rescue line, *La Vie* had drifted much closer to *English Braids*, but the two boats were still far enough apart. He pitched the float, strobe, and line overboard and secured the bitter end to a cleat in the cockpit.

Whenever a wave lifted his bucking boat, Steve stared to windward through the deepening gloom and the mingled spume and rain, trying to gauge Carl's progress. Now he saw the strobed line floating toward him, and he knew the moment was coming when he'd have to leap from his boat. He tightened the straps on his PFD, telling himself to wait until the line was close to his boat. He remembered what he used to tell his students about man-overboard emergencies. Remain calm, he had told them. Do not waste precious energy flailing about in the water. And keep your clothes on; they will slow the loss of body heat. Although the tropical Caribbean was 82° Fahrenheit, Steve knew he might have to spend a long time in the water, and hypothermia was a possibility. He also remembered that he could use his clothes as makeshift buoyancy aids if need be, or wave them for better visibility from the water. It occurred to him that he was thinking clearly; his training was paying off.

Both Carl and Steve watched the line float with excruciating slowness toward *English Braids*. There was no way to make it move any faster. Finally, with the strobe flashing about 20 yards off the stern, Steve saw that it would get no closer; then the gap began to widen. It was time to make his move. He took one last look at *English Braids*, wished her well, and plunged into the water—a true leap of faith for a man who could not swim.

The water must have felt unexpectedly warm. Already soaked to the core from boarding seas and driving rain, Steve was at least now out of the wind. The waves were huge, and he was buoyant with a life jacket on. Floundering, flailing, he somehow made his way to the float. Clutching the light, he felt for the line, found it, and gave two hard pulls. Then he pulled the line to form some slack and lashed it around his waist. Carl had the other end in his hands and started hauling when he felt

Steve's signal. He was surprised how heavy the load was, and how hard it was to pull.

Carl wrapped the line around the unoccupied jibsheet winch and began cranking methodically, slowly pulling Steve toward *La Vie*.

Carl had been thinking about how he would wrestle Steve aboard, and this made him think of Bijou, who was safely ashore in Atlanta. He had a sudden image of the dog, soaked and miserable, shadowing his every move and hunkering down next to his master, getting in the way. It was good the dog wasn't on board. But the stern boarding platform, a required feature for hauling Bijou in and out of the dinghy, was now going to make hauling Steve Rigby aboard a lot easier. Bijou was doing his part. Carl remembered the time when Bijou had jumped too soon from the dinghy and had fallen into the water. Carl had been forced to jump in himself and heft the animal onto the stern platform. If he'd had to use a ladder, he might have lost his dog then.

Suddenly the line jerked tight as a huge wave rushed under the hull and *La Vie* pitched violently away on the wave's backside. If not for the turns on the winch, Carl would have lost his grip on the line. Steve was momentarily out of Carl's sight, but the yank at his end must have been horrible. He reappeared, still doing his best to propel himself, as the wave rolled on to leeward. Still, another wave like that might weaken Steve past the point of assisting his own rescue or even separate him from the line altogether. To make matters worse, the two boats were drifting perilously close together. Carl cranked harder on the winch. Steve must have noticed the same thing, because he was kicking and pulling himself up the line toward *La Vie* as fast as he could.

Carl felt a twinge of panic, a fear not so much of danger as of not knowing what to do. If the boats collided, they would prob-ably both sink. He wanted to put the engine in gear and power out of harm's way, but he had a man in the water. The rescue line, which was jerking from slack to taut with every wave, might snag the propeller and render the engine useless. Even worse, he would risk getting Steve caught in the prop, and instead of saving him he'd chew him to pieces. The rescue was unfolding in agonizingly slow motion. Everything at sea hap-pened so damned slowly. Then he realized it was going to be okay. The boats were close, but *La Vie* was going to drift just astern of *English Braids*.

Then Carl heard Steve calling. He was right there, off the stern, reaching for the platform. He found it and started to pull himself aboard, but had to let go as *La Vie* rose on another huge wave and came crashing down. He disappeared in the cascade of foaming water, and for a moment Carl must have feared that he'd been crushed. But then he reappeared, and Carl heaved on the line. They were in a deep trough. This was the moment, the relative calm, the only possible time to get Steve aboard. Steve hauled himself onto the narrow platform, his considerable strength and agility allowing him to press himself up like a gymnast. A larger, heavier, less fit man would never have made it aboard. Carl grabbed him under the arms, and Steve tumbled over the stern rail and into the cockpit.

Both men were completely spent. They must have embraced, and Steve thanked Carl profusely. Though they were too tired and burdened for conversation, a profound understanding passed from man to man. The only way to savor the essence of life is to nearly lose it. The exhaustion and exhilaration of the aftermath are bathed in a profound humil-ity, a realization that life itself is all that matters. Those who have felt death's fingers on their throats and wriggled free are the lucky ones.

Hauling Steve Rigby into the cockpit of *La Vie en Rose* was the capstone of Carl Wake's life. When other men would have run, he had stayed. When others would have saved themselves, he had saved another man's life. Beyond duty, beyond freedom, he had become, if only for an hour, the man he'd always hoped to be. Surely it must have seemed to Carl as if some force, some unseen hand, had guided him to these storm-tossed Caribbean coordinates on the wrong side of a wrong-way hurricane for the express purpose of rescuing Steve Rigby and glimpsing the shape of his own soul.

Glancing at his watch, Carl was shocked to see that it was not yet nine o'clock. The entire rescue had taken less than 2 hours. He helped Steve below, wrapped him in a towel, and insisted that he lie down. Then he called VISAR and calmly informed them that he had Steve Rigby aboard and that they were abandoning *English Braids* and would continue south to try to get out of Lenny's way. He asked for an update on Lenny, and his euphoria faded with the response. The latest coordinates put Lenny 180 miles west-southwest of St. Croix, with maximum sustained winds between 100 and 105 knots—a Category 3 hurricane. VISAR passed the news of the rescue to the Coast Guard in San Juan. The Coast Guard told Julia that Steve was safely aboard *La Vie en Rose*. Steve Rigby was grateful for the relative warmth and stability of *La Vie*'s cabin, but the radio transmission echoed with a stark finality. His boat was floating alone on dark seas, left to her own all-but-certain fate. Soon they'd have other worries, but for the moment Rigby lamented the loss of his boat and his innocent faith in an ocean that would nurture a sailor's dream.

By the time Carl pulled his sails around and pointed *La Vie*'s bow southward once more, the wind on deck was gusting over 80 knots, and the seas continued to build, reaching 30 feet and higher and breaking more frequently. Carl didn't need the VISAR update to know that Lenny was getting stronger and closer. At 2300 AST the hurricane watch for all of the Dominican Republic was discontinued, and hurricane warnings were posted for Antigua, Barbuda, and Montserrat.

La Vie's position next morning would suggest that Carl kept the boat close on the wind all night, forereaching slowly ahead under a scrap of sail. He may have put her on port tack initially, resuming the southwesterly course he had been maintaining before the rescue, or he may have chosen to struggle eastward on starboard tack, away from St. Croix, then somehow got back to port tack as the night wore on and the wind swung more into the southeast. But his plan remained to get to the south.

Exhausted as he was, it was comforting to hear another voice aboard the boat. Steve was the first person Carl had seen in nearly twelve days. Though the two men were cut from radically different cloth, on this night, as the wind shrieked in the rigging and the boat labored south and the sea's wide horizons contracted to the claustrophobic pinpoint of a lurching cabin, they were lucky to have each other.

TOGETHER

"It is impossible for anyone who has not experienced that most savage of storms, the hurricane, to comprehend its power. Wind ceases to be wind, it becomes a solid. It tears at every crevice, shakes the stoutest structure. Exposed to its full fury, a human finds it impossible to crawl, or even breathe. It lashes as it batters, carrying all before it: solid sheets of water, sand, trees, houses, spars."

Carleton Mitchell, *Passage East*

ALTHOUGH the storm would intensify dramatically during the night, the radio record from *La Vie en Rose* is strangely quiet. Perhaps the two men actually slept. Steve had been hand steering *English Braids* for more than two days without a break. Without a working autopilot, he would have had to take the sails down just to eat or relieve himself. He had endured the stress of his rescue under twin deficits of sleep and nutrition, and in all likelihood he had been in the water long enough to become mildly hypothermic as well. He must have desperately needed food, warmth, and sleep by this time, and Carl, being Carl, would have insisted that Steve get all three.

So, while *La Vie* resumed plodding stoically into the storm at a couple of knots, thrown on her beam ends by occasional breaking seas but still under control, Carl probably took the first watch. Running the engine had put some charge into the ship's batteries, enough for the running lights and autopilot.

There was little to do but endure and worry. He could open the companionway hatch every 15 or 20 minutes, though to what purpose wasn't clear. There was no visibility. If they should meet a ship out there, they would not know until too late, and GPS was their best guide to the proximity of islands or reefs.

Twelve days into his first solo offshore passage, Carl too was exhausted. Now the stress and labor of the rescue left him drained. He had stopped reexamining the assumptions that underlay his determination to continue south into the battering seas. He lacked the will for thought. Like his boat, he was on autopilot. The army teaches its officers not to change objectives in the middle of a mission, and Carl wasn't changing his. He could not have unraveled, at this late stage, that he was struggling toward the more dangerous side of the hurricane. After an hour or so, perhaps Carl too fell asleep.

Or perhaps Carl and Steve alternated short watches, maybe an hour, maybe two. The little information that can be gleaned from *La Vie en Rose*'s limited postrescue radio reports suggests that Steve Rigby recovered from his ordeal with astonishing speed. It was not in his nature to admit that he was not up to the task, any task. He believed he was capable of almost anything, especially a physical challenge. He was utterly grateful to be aboard *La Vie en Rose* and determined to give Carl a much-needed break. Over Carl's objections, he insisted that Carl lie down.

Carl had a lee cloth rigged across the settee berth in the main saloon. During the passage he had done most of his dozing in the cockpit, so in other circumstances it would have seemed almost decadent to lie in a real berth. But the clanging of pots and pans under the sink, the rolling of plates and cups unleashed in the locker above the stove, and the thud of falling books from shelves created a cacophonous accompaniment to each hurricane-force blast. The waves slamming the hull seemed made of steel, not water. To sleep in such conditions would have required an act of will.

Lying in the berth, pinned to the hull by a combination of gravity and exhaustion, Carl must have been thoroughly soaked and unable to stop his body from shivering. Physically he was spent.

Mentally, however, he may have been in a delayed state of euphoria. It had been an unforgettable 12 hours. He was trying to avoid a hurricane that seemed to be stalking his every move. He'd saved a man's life. And he had crew aboard *La Vie* for the first time in many months. All he needed was an hour or two of sleep to make sense of it all.

Covering his ears with a pillow didn't block out the whining wind. The wind in a tropical system comes at a sailor in waves. It begins with a deep groan that signals another blast on its way. Then it pauses, gathering momentum, like an engine revving, and the rigging moans in anticipation. The pitch then becomes noticeably sharper. Suddenly it's a shriek, and the rigging screams in metallic rebellion as a fierce gust shakes the mast and stays. The boat leans over unsteadily, like a drunk walking uphill. Is this the big one? the sailor wonders. Will she keep going over?

But it's almost never the wind that causes a boat to founder. Once the boat heels over far enough, the sails and rig no longer offer much resistance, and the boat's inherent stability reasserts itself. As the gust passes, the boat slowly recovers. The lead ballast in the keel presses downward, and she regains her footing. The deep canyon in the trough between towering wave crests offers a fleeting sanctuary before the next burst arrives. For a few seconds of relief, the shrieking wind recedes.

Every 15 minutes or so while Carl rested, Steve would pull back the companionway hatch, look quickly around, then pull it shut—like a turtle retreating into its shell—before too much seawater sloshed below. The interior was a soggy mess, ports and hatches leaking under the assault of tons of water crashing on deck. Still, compared with the shattered shell of *English Braids*, *La Vie* was like a hotel room.

Steve would then wedge himself behind the navigation station, his feet propped against the bulkhead to keep himself in place. A soft red chart light bathed the teak trim of the cabin in an eerie sepia glow. He fiddled with the SSB radio, listening to the panicked chatter and frequent Lenny updates on Virgin Islands Radio Channel 401. Hearing other voices, even nervous ones, was reassuring, and he monitored every conversation. Steve would become the radio man now that he was aboard *La Vie en Rose*. He had called Julia, and her voice had lifted his spirits and helped rekindle his natural optimism. "Once he was on the other boat, we both thought the worst was behind," Julia would say later. But he'd never been more tired. He must have dozed from time to time.

As *La Vie en Rose* bucked her way south, the wind continued to increase, and the seas were becoming colossal. Commercial ships more than 200 miles away reported 25-foot seas, and in the Anegada Passage, humped up by the southwest-setting current, they would have been in excess of 30 feet. Every so often a wave would catch *La Vie* in the wrong place at the wrong time and lay her over on her beam ends. When these near knockdowns occurred, anything that wasn't lashed in place was launched from the windward side of the cabin like a missile.

The pace of a storm at sea, even a hurricane, isn't the frenzy depicted in a Hollywood film. It is agonizingly slow, and there is a rhythm. After a while a sailor can feel what's coming. A tracer slap on the hull means that the next breaking wave is about to crash over the boat. Steve and Carl learned to recognize the signs and brace themselves whenever thousands of gallons of water were about to cascade across the thin teak and fiberglass deck, shaking the boat to its backbone. Despite the tightly dogged hatches and ports, a torrent of water sloshed into the cabin after each wave.

Carl had no experience with winds and seas of that magnitude. Few sailors do. Not knowing what to expect or how much abuse your boat can take nurtures fear. When it was time for his watch, I am sure he craved a cup of coffee, but lighting the stove was out of the question. Even if he could get the soaked burners to ignite, the kettle would never stay in place long enough to heat up.

If Carl was lucky, a can of Pepsi rolled fortuitously across the soggy cabin sole. He snagged it, wiped it on his shirt, and popped the lid. It exploded, but what was another mess at this point? He'd clean the boat when they were safely in port. He put his mouth over the fountain of foam for a welcome dose of caffeine and sugar. He did love Pepsi. Steve clapped him on the shoulder and disappeared into the bunk.

THE MONSTER'S JAWS

"You weren't your mama's only boy,
   But her favorite one it seems.
   She began to cry when you said goodbye
   And sank into your dreams."

                    Townes Van Zandt, "Pancho and Lefty"

THE weak half light of an indistinct dawn crept over
the Anegada Passage on November 17. The hurricane had intensified all night. Slivers of gray light filtered through roiling
black storm clouds, revealing an ocean in chaos. Mingled
spume and rain had reduced the visible world to a few hundred
yards, within which there was nothing to see but towering,
colliding seas.

An hour before dawn, at 0600 Atlantic Standard Time, a
Hurricane Hunter aircraft had penetrated Lenny's eyewall. The
dropsondes released from the plane registered 115-knot winds
at the sea surface, and the storm's central barometric pressure
was down to 946 millibars. These data, along with the news
that Lenny had angled more to the northeast and that its forward speed had slowed significantly, were reported in the
National Hurricane Center's 0800 update, a clinical description of a building monster.

The report placed Lenny's center at 16.8° north, 65.5° west,
just 53 miles south-southwest of Frederiksted, St. Croix. The

storm's northern eyewall was beginning to batter the island. Winds of 83 knots were recorded at Hamilton Airport before the anemometer blew away. On nearby Maria Hill, an observer reported a gust of 97 knots. Moored boats were thrown onto piers and into one another. Half the boats in the St. Croix Yacht Club would be lost before Lenny moved on.

La Vie en Rose was approximately 40 miles east-southeast of St. Croix and just 110 miles northeast of Lenny's center. The eye of the hurricane was itself 30 to 40 miles across, and hurricane-force winds extended nearly 100 miles beyond the eyewall, enveloping the sailboat.

Somehow during the night, Carl and Steve had clawed 35 miles southeast, directly into the building winds. Those miles into the teeth of a building hurricane—won at the cost of what must have been a brutal battering—testified to the determination of the two sailors and to the seakeeping qualities of Carl's boat. But despite pushing the boat and themselves to the limits of endurance, Carl and Steve had lost the race to the railroad crossing. Lenny's turn to the northeast had come too late. The storm's latest forecast track would place it directly overhead by late afternoon, and now *La Vie* could no longer carry any sail. She was a sitting duck, and when Lenny did overrun them, they would be southeast of the eye, in the strongest winds.

La Vie en Rose was virtually alone in her patch of the Caribbean. The Coast Guard had ordered their cutters south, out of harm's way, and all commercial shipping had been diverted away from what was now forecast to become a major hurricane, possibly even a Category 5. The only other vessel anywhere near *La Vie en Rose* was a black-hulled schooner, and she too was in the fight of her life.

Guillaume Llobregat's decision to skirt Lenny, to let it slip by just to the north of *Frederic-Anne* so that he might hurry back home on the storm's shirttails, now seemed a tragic miscalculation. He must have begun to realize this while plugging slowly east-northeastward during the night, and the 0800 update from the National Hurricane Center confirmed it. Lenny's new track would eventually carry the storm right over St. Martin, but before it reached Llobregat's home and family, it would collide with *Frederic-Anne*.

Llobregat and his mate, Jacques Santos, had spent the night standing 1-hour watches. First one, then the other wrestled the wheel, desperately trying to keep the seas on the starboard quarter and off the deck. As the winds continued to build, they had no option but to keep reducing sail. No sail can withstand hurricane-force winds for long, and by morning they were under bare poles. They were running the engine more for stability than speed, and the propeller was helping to keep the schooner's stern under control. As Lenny drew closer, however, and the wind backed from south to southeast, Llobregat was forced to alter course more and more to the north, which kept the seas on the quarter but was also delivering the schooner directly into the monster's jaws. As of 0800, *Frederic-Anne* and *La Vie en Rose* were probably less than 20 miles apart.

Ocean waves, for all their complexity, are defined by a few simple dimensions: Wavelength is the distance from one crest to the next; wave height is the vertical distance from trough to crest; the period is the time in seconds between the arrival of two successive crests; and the velocity of a wave is inversely proportional to its period. In deepwater swells—waves traveling across water that is at least half as deep as the waves are long—there are consistent and predictable relationships among these dimensions. A typical large ocean swell with a 15-second period, traveling at 40 knots, will have a length of around 1,000 feet. For this to be a deepwater wave, the ocean depth must be at least 500 feet. Such a wave, even when its height is majestic, is no threat to a small boat, which rides over it with ease. But storm waves do not become swells until the wind stops blowing.

Wind-generated waves increase with the strength of the wind, its duration, and the unfettered stretch of ocean, known as fetch, across which it blows. The waves accompanying Lenny had been building for days across 800 miles of open sea. Because the storm had tracked south of the large islands of Hispaniola and Puerto Rico, there had been no significant landmass to interrupt these building seas. According to models developed by the Institute of Oceanographic Sciences in Surrey, England, Lenny's waves might have been in excess of 60 feet high—higher than *La Vie en Rose*'s masthead.

But this does not adequately describe the actual sea conditions Carl Wake, Steve Rigby, Guillaume Llobregat, and Jacques Santos were experiencing. Though the significant wave height—the average height of the highest third of the seas—might have been 60 feet, occasional seas would have been much higher. The highest measured significant wave heights were 50 feet in Hurricane Ivan, a Category 4 storm in the Gulf of Mexico in September 2004, but individual waves as high as 91 feet were reliably measured outside the eyewall, and wave heights inside the eyewall are thought to have exceeded 130 feet. And waves in storms are not the regular, sinusoidal deepwater swells that roll across the oceans hundreds or thousands of miles from the disturbances that created them. Rather, storm waves are a study in chaos.

As Hurricane Lenny approached the Anegada Passage, it first whipped up huge seas from the southwest. Within this wave train, bigger, faster-moving crests overtook and consumed smaller ones, growing larger still. Eventually, under the continuing influence of hurricane-strength winds, some of those crests grew so high and steep that they became unstable and began to collapse, or break. When a crest angle falls below 120 degrees—or, put another way, when the ratio of wave height to wave length exceeds 1:7—the wave becomes unstable and will almost certainly break. In a breaking sea, the nondestructive energy locked in an undulating waveform is transformed into the unleashed mass, momentum, and kinetic energy of tons of white water tumbling from a wave crest at speeds in excess of 40 knots. Swells do not destroy boats, but breaking seas do. No small boat, no matter how sturdy, can withstand a large breaking sea. If it is in the wrong place at the wrong time, it will be broken apart as if made of kindling.

As Lenny approached, the seas from the southwest were followed by seas from the south and then the southeast, and as these wave trains collided, occasionally reinforcing each other, huge breaking seas reared up in every quarter.

To make matters worse, both *La Vie en Rose* and *Frederic-Anne* were encountering Lenny in the worst possible place, over the Saba Bank, a broad, shallow shelf west of Saba Island. The sea bottom south and southeast of St. Croix reaches down to more than 13,000 feet deep, but 40 miles east, over the bank, the soundings rise abruptly from 3,000 to less than 100 feet. Nothing transforms a survivable deepwater wave into a steep, breaking, destructive cascade more effectively than a sudden rise of the ocean floor. When a wave "feels the bottom" in depths less than half its length, the base of the wave is slowed by friction, in effect causing the crest to overrun the base and eventually to break. Even waves that would otherwise have been survivable were turned into weapons of destruction when they started to break on the shallows of the Saba Bank.

Aboard *La Vie en Rose*, Carl and Steve must have talked about what to do next, but there really wasn't much to discuss. There was no way to sail out of Lenny's way, no way even to control the boat. After days of forging south to skirt the storm, *La Vie en Rose* was reduced to being thrown before the storm under bare poles, slowly drifting back to the north. Wave after wave swept over the boat, each one flooding the deck with thousands of pounds of water. The fiberglass flexed and distorted under these loads, allowing water to pour in everywhere, around hatches that were dogged down as tight as a man could dog them. If a hatch gave way, the boat would be swamped before they could fashion a jury-rigged replacement. If the hull or deck gave way, she'd sink like a stone. The bilge pumps were already struggling to keep up with the ingress of water. *La Vie en Rose* moaned and creaked. She was laboring, and it was only a matter of time before she broke up. It was time to ask for help, to call the Coast Guard and have them send out a ship or a helicopter. It was time to leave *La Vie en Rose*, to let her cope with Lenny on her own.

Or was it?

Steve could hope to find another boat in which to pursue his ambition to become a singlehanded racing sailor, but Carl had made a one-time-only emotional investment in his boat and all that she represented. There would be no other. It wasn't a matter of money. Although most blue-water voyagers find insurance to be exorbitantly expensive when available at all, Carl had been able to purchase worldwide coverage for *La Vie* through the United Services Automobile Association, which provides financial services for members of the military. The boat was covered for $90,000. He could replace the boat. But Carl had no insurance on his dream. He possessed neither the naïveté nor the will to begin again. The choice now confronting him must have struck him as bitterly cruel.

The motion in the cabin was violent, and it would not have been possible even to stand up. Braced on the settee, however, Carl could survey his still-floating world: painted white bulkheads with bits of teak trim, tropical fabric on the settee. He had once told me that he was sure a woman had decorated *La Vie*. Somehow this boat, lean and muscular on the outside, feminine within, had brought out the best in him. With this boat he had pursued an uncompromised dream. In this boat he had propelled himself over an ocean, rescued a man in a hurricane, endured a crucible, and found within himself the man he'd always hoped to be. He had made this boat his world, imposed on it his own idealized order, and then in turn been re-created by it.

Listening to Virgin Islands Radio, Carl and Steve must have wondered why they had pressed south into the storm. Reports coming from land and sea indicated that Lenny was barely affecting the Virgin Islands. Carl and Steve had been right there, just a few hours from safe harbor in Tortola. If they had headed north after the rescue instead of south, they'd be in port right now. The irony was as inescapable as the radio chatter. Boats in Charlotte Amalie Harbor were fretting over their anchors dragging in 30-knot gusts. Just to have an anchor down to worry about would have been a wonderful exchange for Carl and Steve.

The winds continued to back. By 0900, 100-knot blasts were coming from the east-southeast, and *La Vie* was aiming roughly toward St. Martin, wallowing with no sails set yet still making forward progress from the force of the wind in her rigging and against her hull. She was near 17.6° north and 63.8° west, approximately halfway between St. Croix and St. Martin and about 30 miles west of Saba. The eyewall was a mere 60 or 70 miles away and overtaking her by the hour. The shrill whine of the winds must have been terrifying. Carl told Steve to call the Coast Guard and put out a Mayday. It was time to abandon ship while they still had an antenna with which to make the call. Every powerful gust that laid *La Vie en Rose* onto her beam ends threatened to carry away the mast and with it their ability to communicate.

According to Coast Guard Lieutenant Commander Jim Munro, by the time Steve broadcast Maydays on *La Vie*'s VHF and SSB radios, the conditions had deteriorated to such a degree that it was impossible to launch a rescue mission. Earlier that morning the decision had been made to ground and lash down all GANTSEC aircraft, including the HH-65 Dolphin helicopters, at Air Station Borinquén in Aguadilla, Puerto Rico. The cutter *Valiant*, the ship most capable of reaching the stricken sailors, had been deployed to smoother southern waters. Munro said later that if Carl and Steve had called just 2 hours earlier, rescue might still have been an option. Despair and deep fear must have clutched the two men aboard *La Vie en Rose* when they heard the Coast Guard's response.

Then there was a ray of hope. A Dutch naval ship hovering near Guadeloupe overheard Steve's calls and offered to help. The radio officer informed the Coast Guard that they would try to reach *La Vie en Rose*, and the frigate began working its way northwest. Julia Rigby was in near constant communication with the Coast Guard, who kept her apprised of the frigate's position. But it soon became obvious that the ship could not reach the stricken sailboat. The conditions were too dangerous; the frigate nearly broached in a monstrous following sea. After an hour they turned back to the south. Rescue was no longer an option.

At 1100 AST, Steve managed to get a call through to Julia. She was his lifeline. He knew that she was in contact with the Coast Guard, with Virgin Islands Search and Rescue, and with anybody who might be able to help them. He desperately wanted to see her again but realized that survival had become a long shot. "He started to cry. For the first time he wasn't calm and hopeful," she said later. "I was crying too. He said that he loved me and that I was the best thing that had ever happened to him. Then he said that things were not going well, that the boat was threatening to break up, and they could not get free of the storm. He told me that they were going to try to get into the life raft, but he wasn't sure they'd make it. Then he told me again that he loved me."

Carl made no personal calls throughout the storm. As he had so many other ordeals in his life, he endured this one privately.

During the early hours of November 17, Lenny had drifted between two midlevel high-pressure ridges, slowing its forward motion to a crawl. When a well-formed hurricane slows down, it usually intensifies, and Lenny was no exception. The 1100 AST advisory from the National Hurricane Center was devastating. Sustained winds were up to 125 knots, with further strengthening likely. Indeed, 3 hours later, sustained winds of 135 knots would be recorded—the borderline between a Category 4 and Category 5 storm. The chances of surviving such a storm are remote aboard any vessel, much less a 42-foot sailboat. Lenny's center at 1100 was at 17.1° north and 65.1° west, with the strongest winds east and southeast of the eyewall. *La Vie en Rose* was 65 miles east and a little north of the center and a mere 20 or 30 miles east of the eyewall.

Now the hurricane had started to move again, traveling northeast at 8 knots. The leading eyewall would pass directly over *La Vie en Rose* in less than 4 hours.

At 1300 AST, Steve again made contact with the Coast Guard, frantic. He had time to say that *La Vie en Rose* was breaking up, then he lost the signal. At 1320 he was able to get through once more. With greater composure this time, he told the radio officer that they were sinking and were going to try to get into the life raft. He gave their position, 17.7° north, 63.7° west. They were 25 miles west of Saba. They had made it off the Saba Bank, but that no longer mattered. That was their last communication.

It doesn't take long for a boat to sink once its watertight integrity has been breached. A 6-inch hole 6 inches below the waterline will admit 500 gallons per minute to the boat's interior, and as the boat sinks the leak rate increases. By the time the hole is 2 feet below the waterline, it allows 1,000 gallons per minute into the boat. Carl's largest electric bilge pump was able to remove just under a gallon per minute at optimal efficiency, and his manual pump, when stroked with the force of a desperate man, could move about a quarter of a gallon per stroke. A furious rate of 100 strokes per minute would have translated into 25 gallons per minute, which was far too little, and anyway how long could anyone keep that up? Once the boat started to sink, it was just a matter of time before the weight of the water overcame *La Vie en Rose*'s reserve buoyancy. "There's not a worse feeling imaginable than knowing the boat is going down and you're going into the water," Alex Bennett says.

The boat's six-man Eurovinyl life raft was designed for off-shore use. It had a full canopy and a small sea anchor that could be deployed to keep it steady in the water. Carl had climbed inside it when it was serviced in Annapolis and had declared it cozy, but that was on a shop floor, not a ravaged sea. Life rafts work better in theory than in practice; the raft is something to be checked off a list when a sailor prepares his boat for a passage, not something he ever expects to use. He may feel safer just knowing his raft is there on deck, but clinging to one on a storm-tossed sea is another definition of torture. Even the stoutest raft is flung about like a toy in a bathtub. The unfortunate people inside are almost instantly seasick, and it doesn't take long for the raft to be swamped, leaving its occupants drenched and shivering. Further, there is no way to propel a life raft. All you can do is sit and worry, hoping that somebody will come to your assistance.

La Vie en Rose's life raft was housed in a fiberglass canister, which was mounted in a stainless steel cradle near the base of the mast. Many cruising sailboats stow their rafts in this position, but it is not the ideal location, requiring a crew member to make his way forward, unstrap the lashings, and either launch the raft from there or carry the awkward 70-pound load back to the cockpit in storm conditions. Another reason not to mount the life raft on deck is that it is prone to being washed overboard. *La Vie en Rose* had repeatedly been swept by powerful waves. In the cabin, Carl and Steve had no way of knowing if the raft was still in its cradle and good reason to suspect that it was not.

Launching and boarding a life raft in calm conditions is

challenging. The sailor is supposed to toss the raft overboard with the painter, or attachment line, secured to the boat. The raft is then inflated by pulling the painter until pressure is felt. At that point a sharp, short yank removes the pin from a CO_2 canister, and the raft begins to fill. Sailors are taught to draw the fully inflated raft alongside the boat and try to board it without entering the water—thereby lessening or at least delaying the onset of hypothermia.

But proper technique was not an option for the crew of *La Vie en Rose*. There wasn't time—the boat was foundering, and the wild seas would never permit such a deliberate procedure. It was impossible to stand up in the cockpit, much less on deck. Assuming the raft was still there, they would have to hastily cut it free, toss it into the water, pull vigorously to inflate it, and hope that it didn't blow away faster than they could swim to it. Carl wasn't a strong swimmer, but at least he could swim.

Carl and Steve would have pushed open the companionway and pulled themselves into the cockpit. The deck had been stripped clean. The spray dodger, the bimini sunshade, the stainless steel bracket with the solar panels and wind generator, and the emergency life ring and strobe light were all gone. It was impossible to stand up without being blown off the boat. Maybe they took a split second to marvel at the emerald, white-capped liquid mountains that surrounded them, or maybe they didn't. Wind, rain, and seas combined to create a blinding salt spray that burned into any exposed skin. Both men were wearing safety harnesses and had stashed emergency beacons, or EPIRBs, into their foul-weather jacket pockets. Carl had his passport in a waterproof bag, along with his wallet and some money. He was wearing a life jacket, but most likely from oversight, Steve may not have been.

At least one of the two men—perhaps Steve, the younger and fitter—worked his way forward to the mast, keeping his lifeline clipped on. Under repeated assault by boarding seas, the journey of just a few yards would have required a supreme effort. There he found the raft—or didn't. If it was there, he either succeeded in launching it or not. And if he succeeded, it either blew away or didn't, and one or both men either succeeded in boarding it or didn't. And within a few seconds or a few minutes, perhaps with one or two witnesses or perhaps with none, the battered hulk of a once-proud sailboat sank from view.

FREDERIC-ANNE was still afloat on the afternoon of November 17. Even amid the steep, breaking seas over the Saba Bank, the black-hulled schooner was miraculously under control. Guillaume Llobregat was the most experienced of the three skippers battling Lenny's ever-increasing winds and seas. He knew his boat intimately; he had sailed her thousands of miles and knew how she responded. When the wind backed into the east, Llobregat and Santos knew they were near the eyewall. If they could survive the next few hours, maybe the worst would be behind them. If they could just keep pushing north into deeper water, where the seas would be less inclined to break, they might yet make it through the storm.

At 1400 AST Lenny was centered at 17.4° north, 64.8° west, 18 miles south of St. Croix and perhaps 60 miles west of *Frederic-Anne.* The hurricane's sustained winds were up to 135 knots, and its central pressure had plummeted to 933 millibars. The northern eyewall had been raking St. Croix since morning, and the storm was moving northeast at 10 knots. Hurricane-force winds extended 75 to 100 miles from the eye, and winds in excess of 35 knots were being recorded as much as 215 miles from the storm. Saba was receiving gusts of 97 knots, with 61 knots in St. Thomas, 80 knots in St. John, and 73 knots in St. Martin. The passenger ship *Maasdam*, located near Guadeloupe, 150 miles from the eye, reported storm-force winds and 20-foot seas.

After steering all night, Llobregat and Santos had no option but to keep manning the helm through the long hours of November 17. Running before the vicious, unrelenting wind required complete and unremitting concentration. Any momentary lapse might allow *Frederic-Anne* to turn broadside to the wind, ensuring an almost immediate capsize and probable sinking. The rudder was under enormous pressure each time the boat skidded down a wave, and that pressure translated to the wheel. Although the steering system—which consisted of the ornate wooden wheel, steel cables, bronze sheaves, and a massive iron rudder quadrant—provided plenty of mechanical advantage, the helmsman needed to exert a constantly changing combination of raw power and quick-handed finesse to keep the boat true to the waves in those severe conditions. At times the helmsman must have felt as if the wheel would surely fail as he spun it wildly one way and then the other to bring the lumbering schooner back on course.

Time creeps in a storm at sea, but eventually twilight approached, a darker shade of gray. No momentary glimpse of wan sunlight punctuated the gloom, and no dash of red streaks crossed the storm-tossed horizon to provide some tenuous hope. The clouds swirled low, smothering even the faintest glimmer of light.

As darkness engulfed *Frederic-Anne*, the engine gasped for air, then shuddered to a stop. The constant rolling may have created an air lock or, more likely, it loosened sediment in the tanks that then clogged the filters. Either way, without an engine, *Frederic-Anne* became sluggish and extremely difficult to control. Then the wheel went limp and the boat stopped responding to the helm. The steering system had failed. It did not take long then for *Frederic-Anne* to turn broadside to the wind. Llobregat scrambled to find the emergency tiller, but it was hidden away at the bottom of a cockpit locker. A cresting wave broke across the decks, *Frederic-Anne* lurched to starboard, and water flooded below. Somehow the schooner righted herself. Jacques Santos flailed at the bilge pump, but the intake was clogged, the pump was useless—and it would not have mattered anyway. *Frederic-Anne* was sinking, and a manual pump was not going to prevent that. The next wave would send her to the bottom.

Jacques Santos would later remember hearing Llobregat shout, "Get the water bottles and the life raft!" Santos hefted the six-man raft into the cockpit. Unlike *La Vie en Rose*, *Frederic-Anne*'s raft was packed in a valise and stowed in the pilothouse. "Now, Jacques, now!" Llobregat screamed, and Santos pitched the raft overboard, clinging to the painter.

The wind lifted the 80-pound raft into the air like a kite. The painter pulled tight, the CO_2 cartridge released, and the raft began to inflate in midair. The polypropylene painter tore Santos's hands and slashed his arms, but somehow he held on. Their survival depended on it. Before his horrified eyes, the floor and canopy of the raft were shredded, leaving what was, in effect, just an oversized life ring. Finally it plunged into the sea as another wave washed over *Frederic-Anne*. She listed hard over, stricken, then hitched, pitching fore and aft, a sign that sinking was imminent. The two men stood on her sturdy bulwark, took one last look at the boat, then plunged into the sea.

For a split second it was reassuring to be in the water and off their sinking ship. The water was warm, the wind was muffled, and the ship provided a lee from the seas. But they were adrift in the Caribbean Sea in the middle of a hurricane. Swimming frantically, they reached what was left of the raft and tried to pull themselves onto it, but as they did a wave pitched it end over end. "The raft went over four or five times," Santos later reported, "and when it finally stopped another giant wave broke right on us. When I came up I never saw my captain again." In the confusion of abandoning ship, neither man had thought to deploy an emergency beacon or strap on a personal flotation device.

Jacques Santos wrapped his arms and legs around the raft tube and hung on. The water hissed all around him, and the waves stripped away his clothes. His skin was instantly irritated from chafing on the rubber sides. He shivered with cold, the notion that the water was warm having long since passed. It required all his strength to hold on, and there seemed little point in persisting. He was sure he would die. But each time he was on the verge of letting go, he found new resolve. He thought about his wife, whom he desperately wanted to see again. The thought that he would not made him angry. He pictured his entire family, and their images gave him strength. Through the dark evening hours of November 17 and into the wee hours of November 18, 26-year-old Jacques Santos clutched the raft, and with it life itself.

A SURVIVOR

"Regions of sorrow, doleful shades, where peace
And rest can never dwell, hope never comes
That comes to all."

John Milton, *Paradise Lost*

Back in England, Alex Bennett was monitoring BBC reports about a faraway hurricane. "When I saw Lenny's storm track on television, I immediately thought of Steve and phoned up his wife." The news Bennett received was difficult to comprehend. Julia told him that Steve was missing at sea. She said that he'd abandoned *English Braids* and been picked up by another boat and that he and another sailor were possibly, hopefully, in a life raft.

"She kept asking me, 'You're a sailor, you must know what they're going through. What are his chances? Could he survive in a life raft?' I tried to reassure her that he might still be rescued, but she was inconsolable. I knew the odds of them making it were not good. Not in a Category 4 or 5 hurricane."

Tyler Pierce of the Offshore Sailing School also spoke to Julia during those horrible hours when nobody knew whether Carl and Steve had even made it into their life raft. "She said the Coast Guard was waiting for the conditions to improve before they'd launch a search but that they were assuming they were in the raft and they were going to do everything possible to find them. She said that it probably wouldn't happen until the next day. She wanted to know if I thought they could survive in a raft in those conditions. I told her that if anybody could it was Steve, and I meant it. She was incredibly distraught, but still thinking clearly. I ached for her and for Steve. It just didn't seem fair."

Shelley Grund received a call from the Coast Guard early on November 18, and the news staggered her: Carl was missing. She couldn't believe what she was hearing. It wasn't possible. She hadn't even known Hurricane Lenny existed. The storm had received little coverage in America's national media, and a Caribbean hurricane does not make it onto the local news in Appleton, Wisconsin. She was told that Carl had rescued another man, and that the Coast Guard was going to do everything possible to locate and rescue Carl and Steve once conditions improved. She learned that the last message from them had been the previous afternoon, saying that they were about to try to launch their life raft.

Once she stopped crying, Shelley put the distressing news out on the Web. From California, to Atlanta, to New Hampshire, to Florida, word went out that Carl was missing at sea. She hoped and prayed that anyone who knew him, and who was part of his e-mail list, would have information that might help the Coast Guard. There were so many questions, and answers were in short supply. Who was this Steve, and how had Carl sailed into a hurricane? She was no sailor. She did the best she could to answer the concerned e-mails that poured in. The next 48 hours would be among the most intense and exhausting of her life.

Lenny slowed again during the night, and the winds dropped slightly. At 0800 AST on November 18, Lenny was centered at 17.8° north, 63.6° west, almost the precise coordinates of Carl and Steve's final call. Maximum sustained winds were 120 knots—still a Category 4 storm. The National Hurricane Center's update began with "EXTREMELY DANGEROUS LENNY STALLS AGAIN NEAR THE NORTHERN LEE-WARD ISLANDS."

Lenny was just 35 miles west-southwest of St. Martin, and the unprotected western shore of that island was being battered by seas riding ashore atop an unprecedented storm surge. Inside crowded Simpson Bay Lagoon—one of the Caribbean's leading hurricane holes—yachts were reporting 6- to 8-foot waves. Anchors were dragging and boats were grounding. The Llobregat family had battened down the hatches on the four houses in their compound. Lenny came ashore directly over them at eight o'clock that evening, but they were on high ground, and although their structures shook with every gust, for the most part they remained intact. Looking below, where the sea was pounding the shore, Jacques Llobregat could not help but think about his son. He had confidence in Guillaume's sailing skills and judgment. He told himself that if anybody could avoid Lenny, it would be Guillaume. "I had a mental picture of him anchored off a lovely island well south of the storm."

According to Lt. Commander Munro, the Coast Guard determined in the late afternoon of November 18 that conditions had improved enough to permit search-and-rescue operations. Lenny was well east of GANTSEC, the Coast Guard Caribbean Command Station in San Juan, Puerto Rico. The island had suffered limited damage, and aircraft were permitted to fly. GANTSEC coordinated nine air searches for the missing sailors that afternoon, and the cutter *Valiant* was ordered to steam back north to assist in rescue operations.

Valiant had maintained a proud service record since her launching in 1967. Classified as a medium-endurance cutter, she was 210 feet long. Although her home port was Miami Beach, she would still be roaming the Caribbean and the Gulf of Mexico as of 2006. She was instrumental in rescuing hundreds of Cuban refugees during the Mariel Boat Lift in 1980. Ten years later she dramatically rescued the crew of the *Mega Borg* when the tanker caught fire off the coast of Texas. In 1996 she was the patrol commander for the Olympic sailing events off Savannah, Georgia. As she steamed northeast on November 18, 1999, her twelve officers and sixty-three crew were experienced in all manner of search-and-rescue operations.

The Coast Guard hoped to find Carl and Steve in the vicinity of 17.7° north and 63.5° west, 40 miles east-southeast of St. Croix and right on the edge of the Saba Bank. An HU-25 Falcon jet searching the area late in the afternoon had picked up a signal from an EPIRB, an emergency position-indicating radio beacon. Both *English Braids* and *La Vie en Rose* had been fitted with new 406 MHz EPIRBs, and Steve had carried the pineapple-sized device with him during his extraordinary rescue. He had also had it with him when he and Carl went on deck to launch the life raft, and it was his signal that the Coast Guard had picked up.

Earlier generations of EPIRBs transmitted unreliable signals with limited range on 121.5 MHz. These signals were occasionally picked up by an earth relay station, but more frequently some commercial or military aircraft that just happened to be flying over the stricken vessel would be the first to hear the signal. The emergency broadcast would then be reported to the Coast Guard, a plane or ship would be deployed, and once they picked up the signal, the beacon acted as a homing device. It is extremely difficult to pinpoint the exact position of a homing

EPIRB, and the effort always becomes a race against time as the beacon's battery loses power.

The 406 MHz EPIRBs offer worldwide coverage and much greater accuracy. The 406 distress broadcast is a stronger, more stable signal that is picked up by satellites, not planes or shore stations. The location of a 406 beacon can be determined within 5 miles on the first satellite pass, and on subsequent passes the position can usually be honed to a couple of miles or less. Newer EPIRBs even incorporate a GPS receiver, allowing the satellite to obtain precise coordinates on the first pass. Each 406 EPIRB is encoded with a unique digital message that identifies the vessel, the owner, and designated emergency contacts. Once the signal is received and the contact number confirmed, the Coast Guard can act quickly to initiate search-and-rescue operations. With 121.5 EPIRBs, the Coast Guard was never sure if a signal was a false alarm. Time and money were wasted on unnecessary searches, while responses to real emergencies were slowed.

Unfortunately, by the time the Falcon jet returned to base in Borinquén, it was too late in the day to commence additional search-and-rescue operations. A nearby British tanker stood by until the Coast Guard told them they were suspending all operations until the next morning, November 19.

When the daylight of November 18 faded, Jacques Santos had been clinging to the life raft for nearly 24 hours. Although the winds had eased somewhat, the seas time and again pitched the raft end over end, pinning Santos underwater for what seemed an eternity before he could finally break the surface, gasping for air, and climb back on top. His skin was raw from salt water, and he had lost all concept of time. Still he hung on through the night of November 18. At daybreak he felt a small surge of hope when the day dawned bright, but his optimism was short-lived.

Soon the clouds moved back in, and a deep despair descended over him. The prospect of another day on the raft was unbearable. It was time to let this end. Then he heard the jet.

JUST after dawn Eastern Standard Time, the Coast Guard called Julia in New York to tell her they had good news. It was even earlier in Wisconsin when a call shook Shelley out of bed. An orange and black life raft had been spotted in the vicinity of where they expected to find Carl and Steve, and they thought two people were aboard. Shelley was ecstatic. The Coast Guard asked if she knew what color Carl's life raft was. She had no idea but thought Carl's nephew Noel might. She passed along Carl's niece Rebecca's number, hoping she would know how to contact Noel. Then she called Rebecca and told her to stand by to hear from the Coast Guard. An hour later Rebecca couldn't stand the suspense any longer and called the Coast Guard. They had good news and bad news.

Falcon jets typically fly with two pilots and three crew members. Tough and fast, these medium-range surveillance planes had, for the most part, replaced the old HU-16 Albatross and C-130 Samaritan prop-driven aircraft by November 1999. The Falcon can fly at dash speed from a few feet above the sea to over 40,000 feet, and it contains an acrylic search window that makes it easier to spot the tiny speck of a life raft on a tumultuous sea. The plane also has a drop hatch for the delivery of emergency equipment. At just before 0900 Atlantic Standard Time on November 19, the Falcon on its way back to base had noticed the raft. The plane was low on fuel, but the crew wanted to be sure the men below knew they'd been spotted. Santos waved frantically as the plane circled five times before heading for Puerto Rico.

Santos was nearly delirious. As the plane flew off, he wasn't sure if he'd dreamed it or if it was real. Soon, however, another plane arrived. Flying low over the raft, it dropped a buoy with water and a radio. It wasn't a dream; his long ordeal would soon be over. Santos was too exhausted to retrieve the buoy, but it didn't matter. Within an hour, an HH-65A Dolphin helicopter was hovering over the raft. These nimble recovery helicopters can fly comfortably at 120 knots for 3 hours and are able to participate in rescue operations up to 150 miles offshore. A state-of-the-art interface between the communication and navigation systems provides an automatic flight control that allows the helicopter to maintain a stable hover a mere 50 feet above a target.

It was obvious to the Dolphin crew that Santos was in no shape to help himself. The decision was made to put a swimmer into the water. Rescue swimmers are the Coast Guard's version of Navy SEALs—skilled, fearless, and in top physical condition. The chopper eased forward and hovered even lower as the swimmer dropped into the water. Regaining his orientation, the swimmer reached Santos just as the lifting harness was lowered. Climbing onto the raft, he secured straps around Santos's chest and legs, then signaled that he was ready to go. Santos rose from the clutches of death, an unlikely survivor, and was flown to the Governor Juan Luis Hospital in Frederiksted, St. Croix.

Apart from serious skin rashes and dehydration, Santos was in remarkably good condition. He called his wife, who was surprised to hear his harrowing tale. She'd assumed he was fine, sailing away in the sunshine to the south while Lenny was walloping St. Martin.

Back in Atlanta, Rebecca learned that the search for Carl and Steve had resulted in the rescue of Jacques Santos. Julia Rigby already knew as much, having stood by on the phone as the mission unfolded. "I could hear the helicopter in the background as the pilot talked to the base. Then I found out there was only one man in the raft, and it wasn't Steve or Carl." The news that the raft was not Carl's, and that there were not two people aboard—just one, a young man from St. Martin—was bittersweet. If one man had survived, others might too. The Coast Guard assured Julia and Rebecca that the search for Carl and Steve would continue. And there was other good news. *La Vie en Rose*'s EPIRB had been positively identified. It was located at 17.6° north, 63.3° west, close to the island of Saba. Two planes and the cutter *Valiant* were on their way to investigate.

In Marigot, Alicia Llobregat received a phone call from Jacques Santos, who told her the entire story of *Frederic-Anne*'s demise. He described how they had been forced to abandon ship, and how, after the life raft pitched over and over, he never saw Captain Guillaume again. Although the Coast Guard was now searching for Guillaume as well, his family knew that without a raft or even a PFD, he had had little chance of surviving. Lenny had battered St. Martin for more than a day before sputtering south. As it moved away from the island, it left behind a pall over the Llobregat home.

Just before noon Eastern Standard Time, the Coast Guard contacted Shelley and Julia again. No trace of Carl or Steve had been found at the latest EPIRB coordinates. They called back 2 hours later to say that the signal was coming from a spot very close to the north coast of Saba and getting weaker. Two planes, two helicopters, and the *Valiant* combed the turbulent seas. By nightfall they still had failed to locate any sign of Carl, Steve, Guillaume, or even any debris from the vessels. Suspending their search until the following morning, they assured Julia, Shelley, and the Llobregats that they would refine their search planning that night and recommence operations at first light on November 20.

The night passed slowly for the families of Carl, Steve, and Guillaume. "I continued to hope," Shelley Grund said, "but I knew the odds were getting longer. I was very active, keeping as many people informed as possible, trying to block out the idea that Carl was dead. There was no sleep that night. I just kept staring at the phone, half wanting it to ring and half not wanting it to."

When it did ring the next morning at 0830 Central Time, the news was not good. The crew of the *Valiant* had found Carl's body earlier that morning, floating 4 miles off the northwest coast of Saba. He was wearing a PFD and had identification. He had been dead for several days. Shelley thanked the officer and put down the phone. Then she cried, releasing in a flood the tears she'd been holding back for two days. Vicariously, Carl's dream had become hers. She had eagerly anticipated his communications. Developing and updating his website had been a labor of love. She had always loved him.

When her tears subsided, she did what she'd been doing for two days. She went back to work. After sending out an e-mail informing everyone that Carl's body had been found, she wrote, "For all of you out there who loved him so dearly, thank you for your love and thoughts during this vigil. He was a true sailor and would have wanted it this way. . . ."

Julia reconciled herself to the understanding that Steve's body would not be found. She found a small measure of peace knowing that he was in the sea, where he belonged. The Coast Guard continued to search for Steve and Guillaume until November 24, when operations were suspended and the case was officially closed.

No wreckage from the three boats would ever be found. They had been swallowed by the sea.

NEWS FROM HOME

"Yet the first bringer of unwelcome news
Hath but a losing office, and his tongue
Sounds ever after as a sullen bell
Remember'd tolling a departing friend."

William Shakespeare, *King Henry IV, Part II*

Y‌ou are free to leave. Sorry for the delay." The blond, English-speaking port captain at Marina Hemingway, who looked more Russian than Cuban, had pedaled his bike to the boat to let us know that, although La Cumbre, the meeting of Latin American leaders, was still in progress, the port was now open and we could begin the complicated bureaucratic waltz of leaving Cuba. "I don't know how long it will remain open," he added, unable to mask his exasperation, "so I suggest you don't delay." We grabbed a taxi to the nearby dollar-only—code for gringo-only—grocery store and hastily loaded expensive provisions aboard. Then we steamed to the staging dock near the marina entrance.

Police, immigration, customs, and health officials all needed to board the boat, sign off on stacks of carbon-copied papers, and collect their fees for dubious services rendered. A few well-placed beers and tots of rum helped grease the wheels, but as we prepared to cast off our mooring lines, the police came back aboard for one last search to make sure we were not smuggling anybody or anything out of the country. They looked in every locker and drawer and under every mattress and hatch. They lifted floorboards and opened lazarettes. It made me wonder about Eddie Pilot's manuscript. Would they have cared if they'd found it aboard? I would never know.

We were instructed to leave immediately after the Guardia Frontera, the police, took their heavy black boots off the boat. I felt a pang of regret as we raced the setting sun past the stone breakwalls, then turned east into the Straits of Florida. Eddie's manuscript would have to wait for a gringo sailor more willing than I to take a risk for him.

I had hoped to get a last Weather Channel update on Lenny's position and forecast track before leaving, but it wasn't possible. I tuned in my shortwave radio just in time to catch the last National Weather Service broadcast of November 17. Lenny had become a monster of a storm and was southeast of Puerto Rico, near St. Croix. Hurricane warnings remained in effect for the Virgin Islands and most of the Leeward Islands but had been reduced to a tropical storm warning for Puerto Rico. What a weird storm, I thought, and wondered where Carl was riding out the blow. I was certain he was in the Virgin Islands. It had been twelve days since he had left the Chesapeake Bay—plenty of time to snug his boat into a marina in St. Thomas. We were bound for Crown Bay, at the west end of Charlotte Amalie Harbor—more than 1,000 miles east— and Carl and I had talked about meeting there. The marina was well protected with new concrete docks, and I pictured *La Vie en Rose* secure in a slip. Knowing Carl, *La Vie* was probably tied up like a fly in a spiderweb. He wouldn't take any chances with his beloved boat.

We endured a difficult passage east from Havana. For three days we pounded directly into steep seas and stiff headwinds, motorsailing to make progress. On day four, the wind died and we continued to motor. Lacking all means of long-range communications aboard, we were completely incommunicado, but on November 21, needing fuel, we made our way into the tiny, carved-out harbor at Mathew Town, on the western edge of Great Inagua Island.

The island looked hot even from miles away. Flat, treeless, and sun blistered, its scarred limestone surface was singularly uninviting. The island is partially owned by the Morton Salt Company, and huge salt pans consume much of the interior. Vast flocks of West Indian flamingos occupy the rest. Humans, an afterthought, hover around the fringes.

After clearing customs, we arranged for a fuel truck to come down from the salt pans to top up our tanks. While waiting, I called home. My wife tried to prepare me. "I have really, really sad, sad news," she began. I first thought something had happened to one of the kids. Sensing my terror, she added hastily, "It's not the girls." I waited, hovering between relief and dread. "It's Carl," she said softly, as gently as possible. "Carl is dead." Then she broke into sobs. "He died in Hurricane Lenny."

I was stunned. How could he have died in Hurricane Lenny? No, it was not possible. He had to have been in port. Little by little she gave me the details, as best she knew, of what had happened. *La Vie en Rose* had been in the eye of the storm, had sunk, and Carl had gone down with his ship. The Coast Guard cutter *Valiant* had found his body. There was going to be a memorial service in a week.

I felt sick. The world was spinning. I had to go. I hung up the phone and staggered back to the boat. We took on fuel and hurried on our way. I didn't want to spend any more time in Mathew Town than necessary. I had to get home. I spent hours perched on the bow pulpit as we headed toward St. Thomas, still days away. I was devastated. An acrid mix of guilt and heartache made me nauseous. The next three and half days were the longest I had ever spent at sea. The ocean was uncharacteristically calm, as if Lenny had sucked away all the wind, but for the first time in my life I saw the sea as my enemy. I kept picturing Carl floundering in the water. The night watches were grueling. His death was my fault.

We reached St. Thomas and tied the boat up at Crown Bay, the marina where Carl and I had scheduled our Thanksgiving rendezvous. My crew, Eric and Bill, took responsibility for securing the boat, and I took the first flight to Miami. My wife and two young daughters met me at the airport, and we sped past our home in Ft. Lauderdale, continuing north on I-95, bound for Abbeville, South Carolina. We gulped our Thanksgiving dinner at an exit ramp Denny's and drove through the night.

EPILOGUE: ABBEVILLE

"Not known, because not looked for
But heard, half-heard, in the stillness
Between two waves of the sea.
Quick now, here, now, always—
A condition of complete simplicity
(Costing not less than everything)
And all shall be well and
All manner of thing shall be well . . . "

T. S. Eliot, "Little Gidding" in *Four Quartets*

THE minister smiled a benediction and glanced at his watch. The service was over. The mourners, some two dozen or so of us, filed quietly out of the chapel. Carl's first wife, Sallie, and his best friend, Sallie's sister Shelley, were there with their husbands. His second wife, Bea, was there too. Dave Kotzebue was there with one or two other West Point friends. Carl's sister Pat's adult children—his only surviving kin—and his fellow sailor Al Davis were there, looking stricken and disbelieving.

Our convoy of cars gathered behind the hearse and plodded past antebellum homes. There was no need for a police escort—motorists stopped to let us pass, and pedestrians lowered their heads in deference. A funeral procession was more than just a traffic snarl in Abbeville; it was a time to show respect, even if the deceased was making his first and only appearance in town. Beyond the town limits we wound our way through the red earth of dormant fields and up into the South Carolina hill country. Eventually we turned off the paved road and followed a dirt and gravel track to a small cemetery. A handful of headstones stood in a clearing among a stand of tall pines. This was the Hester family burial ground, the place where all Hesters, including Sallie and Shelley, would one day be laid to rest. Although Carl and Sallie were long divorced, the Hesters were still his family. This was where he belonged, if he belonged anywhere.

It was raining lightly, and the sky was an ominous, almost hurricane gray. I parked the car, and my young daughters piled out. They were confused by Carl's death and didn't like the idea that he was to be buried in the cold ground. Just two months earlier we'd spread their grandmother's ashes in the steel-blue waters of the Gulf Stream, and that to them seemed a more proper way to treat the dead. They liked the idea that a part of her might make landfall in England and another part in Norway, like messages in a bottle. They assumed that all the dying, like their grandmother, turned to ashes. Burial was a macabre thing to them. They were relieved that Bijou, Carl's dog, had not been aboard in Hurricane Lenny.

I lingered among the gravesites, absently reading names on weathered stones. The chill wind reminded me that we were a long way from the Caribbean Sea. It was less than a week since Carl had been found floating near Saba. I kept imagining that I might wake from this nightmare and find myself at dinner with him. Sipping a glass of Baileys, he would lean back in his chair and purse his lips. Then, as though the thought had just occurred to him, he'd launch into the story of how he had managed to sail into the eye of a hurricane on his first major passage. Smiling, turning his palms out, somehow he'd make it sound appropriate, even logical, as though he had deserved a rap on the knuckles for daring to think he was an offshore sailor. Who was he, after all, to assume that passagemaking would be easy? He was no longer surprised, he would tell me, when expectations were swallowed by realities. In his measured Southern drawl, it would all sound plausible, even inevitable. "It was out of your hands, John," he would say. "There was nothing you could have done, and if you think otherwise, you're giving yourself way too much credit."

But misfortune was one thing. Death was another. Carl hadn't been ready to die. He didn't deserve to die.

The military detail leader's raspy voice pierced the misty air like a bayonet cutting through flesh. I made my way to the tent and joined my family.

"ATTENTION. PRESENT ARMS."

The stone-faced honor guard stood erect, manipulating their rifles with a honed precision that made me uncomfortable. Nobody should wield a weapon with the ease and familiarity of a priest making the sign of the cross. The pallbearers hefted the flag-draped casket onto a lowering sling near the overturned red clay. A bugler stepped forward and sounded the first mournful bars of "Taps." I had failed to anticipate the raw power of a burial with full military honors. Tears streamed down my face.

The rain picked up, and a powerful gust shook the canvas tent. It didn't take much imagination to picture the tent as a sail. The swirling clouds were doing their best imitation of a hurricane. I could not blot from my mind a horrible image of Carl floundering in wild seas, *La Vie en Rose* nowhere in sight. He had a searching expression on his face.

For days I had been asking myself what had become a

meaningless, rhetorical question. Why Carl? His death seemed profoundly unjust. The bugler seemed to be asking the same question as he held the final note in tribute.

Sheets of horizontal rain drenched those of us standing in the back of the tent. I picked up my younger daughter and tucked her head beneath my rain jacket. She asked if a shark had bitten Carl and that was why he was in that wooden box— so we couldn't see what had happened. I kissed her golden head. Her question would have amused Carl. "No, baby, Carl drowned in the big waves caused by the storm."

The flag was removed and crisply folded, then one of the honor guard presented it to Carl's nephew Noel, his nearest kin. Then seven guns exploded in unison—once, twice, then three times. A twenty-one-gun salute. I recoiled after each volley. My kids were terrified. The smell of gunpowder lingered in the air.

"AT EASE." Finally, thankfully, it was quiet again. Carl was laid to rest.

The cold rain streaming down my hood mixed with salty tears. I put my fidgety daughter down and wandered among the stately pines, remembering a letter I had received from Carl just two weeks before he shoved off on his fateful passage. He wrote that too many people were confined by their inability to imagine a life they hadn't experienced, and this simple lack of imagination was the root cause of their misery. Carl was determined not to be one of those people.

He'd done more than just imagine a new life. He'd created one and wagered everything on it. Was the letter a sign that he was feeling confident, or a clue that he was terribly nervous and trying to shore up his resolve? I had never responded, and now I would never know.

Gradually the frightful image of Carl in the sea yielded to a memory of him at the helm of *La Vie en Rose*. We were reaching through the turquoise shallows of the Florida Keys, the sails drawing smartly. His smile was distant, private. Suddenly I was certain that his two years aboard *La Vie* had been among his happiest but also among his loneliest. His expression, so vivid in my memory, reflected both conditions.

The rain was coming down in torrents now, and most people hurried to their cars. I tarried. The surrounding headstones seemed to be whispering some vital message about the conduct of a life and the meaning of a death, if only I could hear it.

Carl believed that all actions were distilled in the end to a stark choice between duty and freedom, but my world was grayer, less clear-cut.

I needed less clear-cut answers.

In Thornton Wilder's novel *The Bridge of San Luis Rey*, five people are flung to their deaths when a footbridge suddenly fails. Providentially spared, Brother Juniper becomes obsessed with why those five souls died and others did not. Was it a divine plan or just chance? He painstakingly researches the lives of the five people. He concludes, finally, that whether they perished by plan or chance is less important than the bridge that ultimately joins those who die to those who live. It is a bridge built of love and memory.

Those who love them remember Carl Wake, Steve Rigby, and Guillaume Llobregat, and in those memories, they sail still. Memory conquers death and reconciles the living. Six years after that sad day in Abbeville, this is the answer I cling to, as if to wreckage in a storm.

All shall be well. Sail on, Ragman.

AUTHOR'S NOTE

UNLESS otherwise noted, distances in *At the Mercy of the Sea* are in nautical miles, and wind speeds and boat speeds are given in knots. A nautical mile is 1.15 land or statute miles, and 1 knot is 1.15 miles per hour. Put another way, a sailboat clipping along at 7 knots is making the equivalent of 8 miles per hour, the speed of a Sunday morning jogger. That, by the way, is exceptionally good going under sail. Winds of 115 statute miles per hour are blowing at 100 knots, and sustained hurricane winds of that speed have much stronger gusts embedded within them. The center of a hurricane with 100-knot rotating, or cyclonic, winds will at the same time be moving—usually at speeds between 7 and 14 knots—much as a top travels across a table while it spins.

Times of key events throughout the book are given in local time—again unless otherwise noted. Local time for the Eastern Caribbean is Atlantic Standard Time. For the most part, four-digit military time is used. Thus, 1 P.M. local time is usually given as 1300 hours.

Like any storyteller pursuing his subjects into a cataclysm they did not survive, I have occasionally had to use informed surmise to bridge narrative gaps. A few words on technique are therefore in order to document why I feel confident this story is accurate in all important respects. I'll begin with Carl Wake.

Carl was a close friend and a talker. I came to know him well from our many long conversations, and from my conversations with his friends and family. I also drew extensively on our written correspondence over three and a half years and from his web log, which he updated on a roughly weekly basis before his final voyage. His log detailed not only his itinerary, sailing conditions, and seamanship failures and successes, but also many of his innermost thoughts. A solo sailor's log—whether a bound notebook or a web log—becomes his mate, and Carl's log was chatty and revealing. Once he cleared the Chesapeake Bay on his final passage, he had occasional communications with other yachts, and the skipper of one boat, *MaRiah*, relayed Carl's position on several occasions to his former sister-in-law, who did his web postings. These positions anchor the narrative as Carl approached the Virgin Islands and Hurricane Lenny.

Descriptions of Carl's navigation, sail handling, and daily routines on that passage are drawn from my six-year effort to reconstruct what might have happened. My retelling is based in part on having sailed with Carl, learning his onboard habits and idiosyncrasies. I spent many evenings aboard *La Vie en Rose*, and I know where he stowed his charts, coffee cups, books, etc. I know how much sail he liked to carry in various conditions, and how he fussed over sail trim. I know what knots he tied, where he kept his spare lines, and how he approached his navigation and the other routine tasks of passagemaking. And I know, from our many discussions, what he thought about heavy-weather tactics. I have also drawn on my own experiences aboard sailboats comparable to *La Vie en Rose*.

I never met Steve Rigby, though I would have liked to. My portrayal of him is based almost entirely on firsthand sources, from conversations and correspondence with family, friends, and coworkers. The reconstruction of events aboard *English*

Braids is anchored in his known time of departure from Guadeloupe, known weather conditions, the characteristics of his boat, and his radio calls together with Carl's. Where I've had to resort to conjecture, the narrative signals as much.

Guillaume Llobregat's family welcomed me into their home, and we spent many hours discussing their son's passion for sailing. I was not able to track down Jacques Santos, and relied instead on several accounts of the sinking of *Frederic-Anne* from the BBC, CNN, and an excellent interview recorded the day after Santos's rescue by Cox News Service reporter Mike Williams. In this interview Santos gave a detailed account of the sinking of *Frederic-Anne* and his subsequent ordeal in the life raft. In addition, Alicia Llobregat described in detail Santos's phone call to her immediately after his rescue, and she confirmed his telling of the sequence of events aboard *Frederic-Anne*.

Lenny was a well-chronicled hurricane, and I drew from many published accounts of the storm's erratic behavior. Lynda Lohr's account in the November/December 1999 issue of *Multihulls* magazine was particularly helpful. The National Hurricane Center's extensive report on Hurricane Lenny, compiled by John L. Guiney, was vital in pinpointing Lenny's movements and intensity.

During the height of the storm, the narrative is centered around positions and radio broadcast times as noted by the Coast Guard in San Juan, the Virgin Islands Search and Rescue service in Tortola, firsthand sources, and published accounts. I worked with Coast Guard officers in Miami and San Juan to access this critical information.

ACKNOWLEDGMENTS

This book would not have been remotely possible without the help of many people. First, I'd like to thank Shelley Grund, Carl Wake's former sister-in-law and long-time true friend. She offered insights into Carl's past and his personality. She also maintained his website and posted his log, which proved essential to the narrative. Sallie Slavin, Carl's first wife, was most helpful. Sue Reynolds provided letters, photos, support, and other information about Carl that nobody else could have. I'd also like to thank Al Davis and Dave Kotzebue.

Pat Rigby and Simon Rigby opened their broken hearts to help me understand something of Steve Rigby, their son and brother, respectively. I'd also like to thank Julia Henick-Rigby for prying open the door to painful memories and providing essential details about Steve and his encounter with Hurricane Lenny. Alex Bennett described what it is like to sail a Mini 650 in calms and storms. His many insights were vital to the book. Christian Pschorr took the time to write a detailed letter about his friend Steve Rigby, and also patiently answered my many questions during several visits. Tyler Pierce of the Offshore Sailing School was also most helpful.

Thanks also to Jean Jacques Llobregat, Jacquelyn Llobregat, Camille Llobregat, and Alicia Llobregat. They welcomed me into their home in Marigot and remembered their son, brother, and husband, Guillaume. It was difficult for them, and I am most appreciative. Thanks also to Roger Petit and Steve Tackling.

I'd also like to thank Lieutenant Colonel Roy Deatherage of the U.S. Air Force Reserve and Lieutenant Scott Barton of the U.S. Coast Guard. Thanks also to Greta Schanen, Steve Minkler, Jack Brennan, Andy Heger, Steve Maseda, Mark Henry, Eric Anderson, and Bill Williamson. I'd also like to thank journalists Lynda Lohr and Mike Williams.

This book began as a magazine article in *Cruising World* magazine. Former editor Herb McCormick had the courage to commit to a long, rambling article and encouraged me to wrestle it into shape. Herb and I left Elaine Lembo the unenviable task of final editing, and I appreciate her hard work and enthusiasm.

Writer and sailor Peter Nichols was invaluable to the book. He read the manuscript with great and careful attention, and like a skipper with a deft touch on the helm, kept it on course when I frequently lost my way. He would likely cut the previous analogy, but I can't thank him enough for his efforts. He has an open invitation to sail aboard *Quetzal* whenever his schedule permits.

Jonathan Eaton's commitment to the book was unwavering. He is not only a brilliant editor and a talented writer but also possesses a unique mixture of patience and tenacity. It was a pleasure working together and most of what is good about the book should be credited to Jon; what's not, is surely my own doing. I'd also like to thank Margaret Cook, editing manager, and Molly Mulhern, director of editing, design, and production, who were incredibly supportive. Each time they pored over the latest manuscript with keen eyes, they offered valuable suggestions—subjecting me, however, to several rewrites.

Finally, heartfelt thanks to my wife, Tadji, who set everything in motion in St. Augustine, and to Narianna, Annika, Nicholas, and Alex for weathering the writing of this book.